HUMAN RIGHTS AND CH

Legal, Philosophical, and Politic

Human Rights and Chinese Values

Legal, Philosophical, and Political Perspectives

Edited by
Michael C. Davis

Contributors

Michael C. Davis, Du Gangjian, Eliza Lee,
Claude Lefort, Christine Loh, Margaret Ng,
Song Gang, Anna Wu Hungyuk,
Yu Haocheng, Zhu Feng

HONG KONG
OXFORD UNIVERSITY PRESS
OXFORD   NEW YORK

Oxford University Press
Oxford New York
Athens Auckland Bangkok Bogota Bombay
Buenos Aires Calcutta Cape Town Dar es Salaam
Delhi Florence Hong Kong Istanbul Karachi
Kuala Lumpur Madras Madrid Melbourne
Mexico City Nairobi Paris Singapore
Taipei Tokyo Toronto
and associated companies in
Berlin Ibadan

Oxford is a trade mark of Oxford University Press

First published 1995
This impression (lowest digit)
3 5 7 9 10 8 6 4 2

Published in the United States
by Oxford University Press, New York

British Library Cataloguing in Publication Data
available

Library of Congress Cataloging-in-Publication Data

Human rights and Chinese values : legal, philosophical, and political
perspectives / edited by Michael C. Davis.
p. cm.
Includes bibliographical references (p.   ) and index.
ISBN 0-19-586782-3
1. Civil rights—China. 2. Human rights—China. 3. Civil rights—
Hong Kong. 4. Human rights—Hong Kong. 5. Civil rights—Cross-
cultural studies. 6. Human rights—Cross-cultural studies.
I. Davis, Michael C., date
JC599.C6H85 1995
323'.0951—dc20 95–12257
CIP

Printed in Hong Kong
Published by Oxford University Press (China) Ltd
18/F Warwick House, Taikoo Place, 979 King's Road,
Quarry Bay, Hong Kong

Contents

Preface

Western ideas of human rights in China are generally influenced by harsh images of China's military crackdown at Tiananmen, the numerous arrests of dissidents, and the earlier, more horrific activities of the red guards during the Cultural Revolution. While these events and activities may shape the Chinese human rights debate, they do not reveal the full complexity of the human rights discussion in China, nor of the components of this discussion which often serve as catalyst for such tragic events. Although China appears to be a monolithic force of resistance to human rights, there is, in fact, a diverse public debate on these issues among and between Chinese people and the Chinese government, often conducted at personal risk to its participants. Through a series of essays by leading Chinese, Hong Kong and other scholars and political figures, this volume seeks to reveal and examine some of the ideas that are shaping this debate.

In recent years this human rights debate has been a centrepiece in the relationships between China and Western developed countries. While Western governments and organizations have sought to promote human rights in China, the Beijing government has aggressively resisted the imposition of these Western values. China has continued harsh human rights policies in the face of both domestic and external criticisms.

A more open debate centred on the issues of Chinese versus Western values has become apparent in the last decade, leading up to and following the political demonstrations of 1989. During this period, the Chinese government has actively sought to advance a rival conception of human rights which it asserts is more compatible with China's historical conditions and cultural values. This conception promotes subsistence, developmental, and collective rights over individual rights.

This official Chinese view was recently the subject of intense diplomatic posturing in the processes surrounding the United Nations World Conference on Human Rights, held in Vienna in June 1993. The so-called 'Asian view' advanced at the Vienna meeting was presented in the 1993 Bangkok Declaration, issued in the Asian preparatory meeting to the world conference. In this Declaration, China joined other Asian governments in resisting the imposition of Western human rights and values on Asia. The Declaration states that universal standards of human rights do not override unique Asian regional and cultural values, the requirements of economic development, and the privileges of sovereignty. Although Asian governments accepted that universal standards might sometimes be applicable, Asia remains the only part of the world without a regional human rights convention. This official stance was met with some resistance from the more progressive Asian governments and was challenged by the international and regional non-governmental organizations (NGOs) which met at the same time in Bangkok and Vienna. Ultimately, the Bangkok Declaration was rejected at the June 1993 United Nations World Conference on Human Rights.

China's current developmental processes should be placed in the regional context of East Asia. Even official Asia demonstrates developments contrary to the Bangkok Declaration. While twenty years ago the East-Asian region seemed almost single-minded in its focus on economic development, there has recently been a perceptible shift in emphasis to processes of political reform. Human rights is a major theme in this political discourse. Several governments in the region, such as Taiwan, Japan, South Korea, the Philippines, and Hong Kong, have made substantial political improvements. However, China — along with Malaysia, Singapore, and Indonesia — has continued to place stability and power above human rights, and has resisted the demands for political reform.

The topic of human rights may be considered both by addressing the major rights involved and by considering the underlying political, cultural, philosophical, legal, and economic values which cut across the human rights spectrum. This volume explores the latter aspects, though specific rights inevitably represent a subsidiary concern. The approach taken throughout is a dialogic one, which seeks to engage the reader and invite further exploration. The essays focus on China and, to some extent, Hong Kong; Taiwan and Tibet are not included. These essays make no attempt to exhaust the topic. They seek merely to expose the rich debate beneath the already well-documented official stance, and to explore alternative views.

Michael C. Davis

Acknowledgements

After several years of conducting an annual seminar on human rights in Asia, I have come to realize the need for a concise set of essays on human rights to introduce students and others to the fundamental issues in the Asian human rights debate. I would therefore like first to acknowledge the contributions of my students of the past several years to my conceptualization of this project.

Furthermore, in 1993 I was fortunate to work with colleagues in the Chinese Law Programme at the Chinese University of Hong Kong, the Goethe-Institut Hong Kong, and the French Centre on Contemporary China in Hong Kong in organizing the November 1993 Symposium on the Concept of Human Rights in Europe and Asia. This symposium attracted wide interests and served as a workshop stimulant to the essays subsequently written for the current volume.

As this book winds its way through the final editing process I have had the good fortune to serve as the 1994–1995 Schell Senior Fellow at the Orville H. Schell, Jr. Center for International Human Rights at Yale Law School. I appreciate the Center's contribution to my efforts to finalize this book. While in the North-East, I have also kindly been accepted as a part-time visitor at the Center for Human Rights at Columbia University. Their allowing me to participate fully in the numerous activities of the Center has contributed immeasurably to this effort.

Finally, I offer my appreciation to my research assistant, Ms Venus Ng Poling, who helped prepare the manuscript, and to Mrs Elizabeth Lee, who helped at various stages of this effort. The United College of the Chinese University of Hong Kong and the Chinese Law Programme, respectively, provided the financial support for these staff efforts. Furthermore, with the same financial support, much appreciated translation assistance was provided by Ms Helen Choi (Yu Haocheng essay) and Ms Venus Ng Poling (Zhu Feng essay).

Essayists:

Du Gangjian	People's University of China
Michael C. Davis	Chinese University of Hong Kong
Claude Lefort	Institute for Advanced Studies in Social Science, Paris
Eliza Lee	Chinese University of Hong Kong
Christine Loh	Hong Kong Legislative Council
Margaret Ng	Barrister and Journalist, Hong Kong
Song Gang	Chinese Academy of Social Sciences
Anna Wu Hungyuk	Hong Kong Legislative Council
Yu Haocheng	Columbia University (Visiting Scholar)
Zhu Feng	Beijing University

Part I
The Human Rights Debate

Chinese Perspectives on Human Rights

Michael Davis

Recent years have witnessed an explosion of political discourse concerning human rights in China and Asia. This discourse may be viewed as an ongoing discussion within the Asian community about human rights values. Embodied in the term 'human rights values' is the notion of a principled commitment to what we generally characterize as human rights. The modern content of the term 'human rights' is much debated but, on a general level, has been variously argued to include within its purview such concepts as civil and political rights, economic, social, and cultural rights, and notions such as self-determination and sovereignty. The concept of human rights is the focus of this book. Various assertions concerning the terms 'philosophical content' and 'practical application' are discussed throughout this volume.

Within the Asian discussion of human rights, the Bangkok Declaration,[1] which is to some extent a stimulus for the present volume, is particularly notorious for its attack on the belief that human rights standards can and should be applied equally in every country. The Asian governments which supported this declaration argue that cultural and socio-economic differences among countries render the notion of 'universal standards' for the protection of human rights undesirable, if not impossible. This argument concerning the applicability of universal standards is, in particular, the focus of this book and the current essay.

While the rejection of the applicability of universal standards of human rights is just one part of the Asian governments' view of human rights, it is particularly consistent with the official Chinese policy in this area. This aggressive posture serves to mask more serious Chinese introspection. Many contemporary Chinese and other supporters of universal standards, whether they base their arguments on classical liberal views about the nature of man or on arguments about the evolving convergence of values in the world community, have seriously challenged the official Chinese view. At this juncture it is useful to explore the diverse elements of this Chinese introspection and consider the theoretical implications of this important debate.

Many Chinese scholars and political figures have begun to grapple with the difficult human rights issues which have accompanied modernization and political and economic development. While attention often focuses on the important role the world plays in addressing concerns over China's human rights practices, there is little awareness of the seriousness of this discussion within the Chinese and Asian political communities.

It is important to note that, in contrast to the human rights debate in developed Western countries, the Chinese debate is not merely about fine-tuning an existing human rights regime. Given the rather extreme political repression in China, Chinese reflection often turns to basic questions about human rights values, including questions about the sources of such values and their compatibility with contemporary Asian society. If one looks beyond the rather dire Chinese human rights record of recent years and considers the world of ideas in China as an indication of emerging values, there is room for some optimism that human rights conditions and protection in China may eventually improve.

The Chinese human rights discussion engages scholarly and political circles, as well as the community at large, and it involves both domestic and external elements. This essay will consider some of the parameters of this discussion and highlight some of the issues raised. The other essays in this volume expose the contours of this debate in much greater detail and provide a sampling and analysis of the contribution of Chinese and other thinkers to our late twentieth-century struggle with the questions of human rights and human dignity.

Both this essay and the current volume focus primarily on the underlying questions concerning the nature of human rights and their application, rather than on specific rights guarantees. The latter is addressed to some extent as a subsidiary topic. A starting point for the present analysis is to identify a paradigm by which to engage the subject.

Human Rights Discourse

Many of the conflicts in modern Asia, including China, revolve around the constitutional course a country should take and the resultant commitment to democracy and human rights such a course entails. These disputes often raise fundamental questions concerning political and cultural values. These values range from the modern values of constitutionalism and human rights to traditional cultural and political values, as well as to stability and order, which are thought in the Asian context to have implications for economic development. Difficult questions concerning the alleged conflict between these various values and human rights have often arisen. At the same time, constitutional development in the Asian context has important implications for the development of institutions and the prospects for conflict resolution, peaceful transformation, stability and, more generally, for modernization.

To understand the Chinese and Asian struggle with modern constitutional values and human rights, one must begin with a proper theory concerning the processes of constitutional and human rights development. Such a theory, in my view, should be communications-based. Essentially, we must ask who is saying what, with what meaning, with what purpose or values, through what channels, with what effect, etc. Every communication is subject to such variables as the power and authority of the speaker, the institutional setting, and the receptivity of the audience, as well as less tangible elements such as merits, clarity, and affection. In the area of human rights, such communications often pit the power and authority of officialdom against the voices of dissent. For example, officials may tout such concerns as national security, stability, and order against the claims of free speech and due process of law raised by those in dissent.

The approach taken here assumes that human rights values, whether local or universal, are developed in the context of institutions and processes and the dynamics between them. Values describe processes and institutions, and give meanings to them. In turn, evolving processes and institutions may define, and sometimes confine, the possibilities for the transformation of ideas and values. In these senses, freedom and democracy are both values and institutions, ideas and practices.

Many contemporary theories on constitutionalism and human rights have emphasized the role of communications — institutional, personal, and otherwise — in the evolution of human rights values. These include, for example, the now classical theory of Alexander Bickel, the so-called 'New Haven School' in international law, and even contemporary critical theory.[2] The first focuses on constitutional theory, the institutions of constitutional judicial review, and the processes of discourse about important public concerns in a more fully developed system; the New Haven School focuses on communications in the international constitutive process and on how 'inclusive' (a term preferred to 'universal' or 'international' as reflective of participation in world order processes, generally contrasted with matters of 'exclusive' concern left to determination by individual territorial communities or states) commitments may arise out of the competing claims across various world boundaries; while the latter studies critically the processes of discourse on a philosophical level. All are ultimately concerned with questions of language, meaning, and effect.

Several essays in this book have likewise emphasized the importance of communications and politics to the development of an appropriate human rights commitment. This is true both from a more traditional view of politics, as discussed by Zhu Feng and Margaret Ng, and from the standpoint of contemporary critical analysis, as reflected in the essay of Eliza Lee. The latter essay especially provides a starting point for considering the contemporary beliefs and arguments and the processes for developing human rights values discussed in the present essay and throughout this book. Even the traditional liberal theory discussed by Margaret Ng, which advocates autonomy and pluralism as a means to enrich public discourses, leaves room to assign more precise contemporary meaning to fundamental human rights.

In most developed Western countries, formal constitutional and human rights discourse and development are well documented and accessible. In common law countries, such as Canada or the United States, as Bickel's institution-focused theory suggests, much of the human rights debate may eventually find its way into case law. In the civil law world or in hybrid legal cultures, such as the larger Europe, though the systems of legal/constitutional decision may be different, formal constitutional or human rights discourse is accessible through judicial and administrative decisions or through formal channels of legal exploration. Beyond such official reflections, the interpretations of academic discussion are reasonably accessible.

But in Asian countries such as China, constitutional and human rights discourse may be more scattered and less formalized. It is also less accessible due to the underdevelopment of constitutional legal processes and to the presence of more severe political constraints. Nevertheless, the student of constitutional and human rights development in Asia will find that, in spite of such constraints, there is a lively discussion of human rights taking place. He or she will also find that much of the vocabulary of this discussion is familiar, though the shades of meaning of the various terms used may be coloured by regional differences.

Familiarity with the rich public discussion of human rights issues evident in numerous official pronouncements, laws, and declarations (including the Bangkok Declaration) and in scholarly opinions, including those in this book, is particularly helpful because such materials introduce the student to the vocabulary of the Asian debate on human rights. This Asian discourse may eventually give us a new platform from which to view difficult human rights issues in the larger world. The cultural dimensions of human rights attitudes and practices, long of concern in Asia, have become an important theme in the recent multi-cultural Western human rights debate as well. The argument often advanced, generally characterized as the cultural relativist position, is that traditional or non-Western cultures are severely threatened by the introduction of largely Western human rights values and that such human rights values have little or no application in non-Western societies. This is a predominant theme in the Bangkok Declaration.

It seems important, when considering the role that culture plays in the evolution of human rights, to bear in mind that 'culture', from the standpoint of the communications approach, is not a totally exclusive or static concept. The discursive paradigm includes the idea that different cultures may develop shared values through intercultural exposure and discourse and that such processes may become the vehicle for the evolution of 'universal' human rights standards.

Some may argue that a discursive or communications-based approach suffers from the opposite difficulty from that of the cultural relativist position. That is, instead of imposing the accepted values of one culture on another (criticized by those who embrace the cultural relativist position), a communications-based approach leaves the door open to the acceptance of practically any values, even those declared by a dictatorial regime. While every aspect of this philosophical debate cannot be explored in this essay, suffice it to say that such an approach is not so open-ended. First, the discursive model presumes that the process of developing values related to human rights is shaped by existing historically structured conditions. Second, 'values' under this paradigm are not merely legislation subject to instant change by fiat; they are by definition principles to which societies have a strong commitment, and are evolutionary in nature. Third, the discursive process can be successful only where there is freedom of expression, that is a free flow of information and unrestricted intellectual exchange. As was recognized very early on in liberal discourse (see the essays of Margaret Ng and Claude Lefort), those principles or values which impede discourse and value development are to be resisted.

What distinguishes this approach from liberalism is that rather than human rights values being perceived to have a metaphysical origin with man in the state of nature (this presumption is both the core of the liberal paradigm and of one of the branches of the universalist human rights argument noted above), they are perceived to originate in the discursive community (be it local or international) itself. It could well be that a discursive community embraces liberalism or that it does not. It may even be that the community will, over time, drift in directions which threaten important current values, or even the dialogic process. Our dialogic consciousness, however, represents the best safeguard. Futhermore, as observers, we may endeavour to understand this community's disposition in terms of discourse about values rather than in terms of the metaphysical arguments the community itself embraces, whatever the source. Beyond the values that seek to maintain the discourse, such as those relating to the autonomy of the individual, pluralism, freedom of expression, and democracy, modern discourse, on a practical level, reflects a wide range of options open to communities in giving specific content to human rights, covering the entire spectrum of public and cultural affairs.

Much of the political discussion in Asia is explicitly about the evolving political meaning of constitutional and human rights institutions and values. This may come from human rights activists attacking the government or from political leaders trying to justify their policies in terms of human rights. These statements may appear in international declarations (such as the Bangkok Declaration), constitutions, legislation, and white papers or, less formally, in peace charters, the reports of non-governmental organizations (NGOs), and human rights manifestos, or otherwise in academic, legal, or interpersonal discourse. These and other sources are considered below, and in the other essays in this volume.

Human Rights in China

In the Chinese context, there are many theories and explanations offered both by government and individuals concerning human rights development. As with most modern countries, inquiry concerning China can begin with the formal constitutional/legal structure. Such inquiry reveals what Du Gangjian and Song Gang call 'human rights nihilism' (a constitutional/ legal culture which both theoretically and practically offers little or no protection for human rights); the observer must usually move beyond formal legal documents to public pronouncements, official or otherwise, and general discussion to get a better grip on the current Chinese thinking in this area. In considering the various claims that surface, one should also consider the severe constraining factors inhibiting this discourse evident in the periodic crackdowns on human rights scholars and activists.

Though the Constitution of the People's Republic of China contains a rather long list of the standard human rights guarantees that are claimed around the world, observers are usually struck by the absence of strict enforcement. One salient feature of Chinese government that would appear to explain this is the absence of a system of constitutional judicial review of legislation or administrative acts. The Chinese Constitution, under Articles 62 and 67, is instead interpreted directly by

China's legislative body, the National People's Congress (NPC), or its Standing Committee. This interpretation is theoretically carried out through enactment of laws, in effect imposing no restraint on the legislature. The problematic absence of adequate legal safeguards is discussed in some detail in Yu Haocheng's essay. Such laws as do exist, to the extent that they are implemented at all (and they often are not in areas where political interests are paramount), are the only conceptual constraint on administrative officials.

Given, in addition, the absence of competitive democratic elections, the government, in practice, experiences little formal constitutional constraint. China has only recently instituted an electoral system in which there are more candidates than legislative positions. The leadership of the Communist Party is constitutionally mandated. Though eight other parties do exist, and have existed throughout communist rule, this is not a genuine multi-party system, as such parties are required to submit to Communist Party leadership.

This system likewise permits little private resistance or criticism. The Chinese Constitution mandates in Article 51 that the citizens' exercise 'of their freedoms and rights may not infringe upon the interests of the State, of society and of the collective, or upon the lawful freedoms and rights of other citizens'. This provision allows the government to resist the claims of freedom of expression raised by those who have been severely critical of the government and are charged with crimes relating to their political activity.

Though freedom of speech, of the press, and of assembly are guaranteed in Article 35 of the constitution, the press also offers little challenge to China's leaders. This is largely due to government or collective ownership of the press nationwide and to a media ethic, rigourously enforced, which emphasizes the propagandistic role of the press and strict official secrecy. Although the government's control was flaunted by several newspapers during the 1989 student demonstrations, which included reporters from the *People's Daily* (China's leading newspaper) marching in the square and publishing unauthorized reports, the government quickly restored control after the June 4th crackdown.

This propagandistic role contrasts sharply with Western notions of free speech: truth-seeking and enriching or facilitating public debate.[3] Under China's model, the government is presumed to know the truth, and the media's role is to spread this government information (though there is some scope for the media to act as ombudsman, and the media sometimes becomes a factional tool in internal party power struggles).[4] A breakdown in public order usually reflects the media's failure to 'educate' the populace.

Professors Andrew Nathan and Randle Edwards have emphasized several characteristics in China's modern human rights tradition: rights are not inherent in humanhood as under natural rights doctrine but are created by the State; rights provisions will generally be worded in the positive, as an express grant; greater emphasis is placed on welfare rights while political rights are more restricted; rights are juxtaposed with duties, a sort of contingent notion of rights; instead of rights being a limit on the State, the State's interests are often a limit on rights; and rights are generally subject to restriction 'according to law'.[5]

In spite of these obstacles, perhaps under public pressure, there is some government movement away from complete human rights nihilism. On a formal level, while still not acceding to the two general international human rights covenants (including the International Covenant on Civil and Political Rights and the International Covenant on Economic, Social and Cultural Rights which are generally viewed as the backbone of the modern international human rights regime; for a discussion see the essay of Christine Loh), the government has declared its adherence to the Universal Declaration of Human Rights, the 1948 resolution of the United Nations which was the first major codification of international human rights standards. It has also recently agreed to various specific international human rights treaties respecting, for example, torture and discrimination against women. On the legislative front it has enacted many laws on legal procedure, protection of the rights prisoners, and the economy and recently enacted the Law for the Protection of Women's Rights and Interest, though the latter is alleged to be very paternalistic.[6] As with the constitution, the problem of the lack of enforcement undermines adherence to the spirit of these laws and commitments.

An even more striking feature of the slight shift away from the nihilist position is the government's behaviour in the face of the human rights challenge. While continuing to crack down hard on dissidents and labour activists, as well as journalists, the government has demonstrated an increasing tendency to attempt to justify its policies in human rights terms. In doing so it has embraced *de facto* the standards it often rejects on policy grounds. The government has been increasingly called upon to explain itself to the Hong Kong and foreign press (the same press which it persists in intimidating through arrest and expulsions) and to foreign governments and human rights NGOs. This expanding dialogue includes frequent press briefings and, on a more formal level, official human rights policy pronouncements, such as officially sanctioned press commentary in the mass media, the various white papers on human rights,[7] and the Bangkok Declaration.

The discrepancy between the Chinese formal nihilist human rights ideology and these justifications increases the calls for explanation and further justifications. Meanwhile, domestically, the dichotomy between these justifications, pronouncements, and laws and the actual practices tests the Chinese people's confidence in their own government. Both scholars and the public are paying more and more attention to this inconsistency. In addition to intellectuals, labour has also been particularly restless.

Intellectual Discourse Concerning Human Rights Values

Many private voices in China have challenged and supplemented official government pronouncements. As discussed by Yu Haocheng, these voices were heard rather early on in the period of communist rule. Early writings tended to be very critical of Western bourgeois notions of human rights and sought to develop socialist theory. Mainland scholars Du Gangjian, Song Gang, and Zhu Feng, in their essays in this book, all recognize the importance of socialist human rights theory in the development of human rights in China, as does Yu Haocheng. Attempts have been made to understand Marxist theory on human rights.[8]

The Chinese socialist critique of human rights is significant if one notes that a form of traditional feudal society, guided significantly by elitist Confucian principles, was operative until very recently in China. Recognizing that Confucianism has a strong humanistic component, recent scholarship has sought to identify human rights ingredients as well. It is important that this is taking place in a period of revival of Confucian values that cuts across East Asia and represents a significant backdrop to the cultural relativist strains in the Bangkok Declaration.

While others have argued the case for seeking human rights values in Asian traditional culture,[9] Du Gangjian and Song Gang have made a significant contribution in this respect in their essay in this book. These writers have not taken the rather perilous path of trying to prove that traditional Confucian society had a highly developed human rights regime. They have sought instead, through careful analysis of Confucian writings, to identify many strains in classical Confucian thought that were consistent with the elements of modern human rights values. They seek to dispel the extreme nihilist argument that human rights are simply a Western invention completely alien to Chinese soil. By this reasoning they seek to refute the cultural relativist argument that there is a cultural obstacle to human rights implementation, as was advanced in the Bangkok Declaration.

They argue that classical Confucianism — as opposed to more recent practice — contained elements that encouraged actions of citizenship, criticism of government, freedom of speech, resistance to authority, and individualism, to name a few examples. At the same time they acknowledge that Confucianism was élitist and undemocratic. In this sense they accept the view that democracy is alien to Chinese soil, while advocating that when it is practised consistently with traditional values it must embody genuine choice and open elections. The authors urge that because of these value systems, human rights can be established ahead of democracy.

This view contrasts to some extent with socialist ideas of democracy leading society to the promise of human rights, and with the views expressed in the essay of Zhu Feng, who sees political development as the avenue to human rights in Chinese society. Socialism, though its democratic elements have yet to be realized in China, certainly encourages the notion that the government must be responsive to the needs of the masses and advances egalitarianism as one of its objectives. Zhu Feng's critique seeks to expand on this promise within the limits of current economic reform. For the Chinese intellectual today this search for the proper path forward is a balancing act between the commands of practical economic and political reality and the ideals of human rights.

Many dissident elements in the Chinese intellectual community have, at great personal risk, exceeded the strictures of this balance, severely challenging the leadership's attachment to the mandates of political reality, tradition, and Marxism. It is important to note at this juncture that many so-called dissidents in China are avowed Marxists. But many, especially on the human rights front, have embraced more clearly liberal notions of democracy and human rights and encouraged the application of universal standards. As revealed in the essay of Yu Haocheng, this may or may not involve a complete break with socialism.

The slight official shift off of the human rights nihilist position noted above has been in no small part due to pressure from intellectuals in China. While the student-led democracy movement in Tiananmen Square in 1989 is the most well-known example, there have been others, including the 'Hundred Flowers Campaign' in 1957 (when Mao set an anti-rightist trap by inviting intellectuals to speak out, to which they responded in droves by criticizing the Party, only to be arrested and punished) and the 'Democracy Wall Movement' in 1978–9 (a more truly spontaneous movement in the early days of reform which also resulted in arrest; the most prominent arrest was of Wei Jing Sheng, still an active dissident). The values — justice, public accountability, and the right openly to express ideas — promoted in these movements increasingly penetrated beyond intellectuals (earlier cases) to find an audience in the masses (Tiananmen), at least in the urban areas.

Less known than these campaigns and mass movements are the more subdued attempts by leading intellectuals, both within and outside the government, to encourage political reform. In the mid-1980s scholars at People's University conducted political surveys on the role of the media and encouraged media reform. In the late 1980s, under the leadership of former Communist Party Secretary General Zhao Ziyang, government and private think-tanks (including one led by recently-released dissident Wang Juntao, who had been arrested for being the 'black-hand' behind the 1989 democracy movement) encouraged electoral reform and press reform. At the same time, more liberal factions within the ruling elite in the government were promoting similar political reform, though this effort appeared to fail in late 1986 and early 1987, culminating in the deposing of the then Communist Party General Secretary Hu Yaobang. In February of 1989 forty intellectuals led by astrophysicist Fang Lizhi wrote a letter demanding political reform.

More recently, in March of 1994, seven intellectuals, led by liberal reformist Professor Xu Liangying, sent a similar letter to President Jiang Zemin demanding that the government release 'all citizens detained because of their thoughts and expressions of opinion'.[10] In the letter, entitled 'An Appeal for the Improvement of Human Rights in Our Country', the writers asserted, 'The right of the freedom of thought and the expression of opinion is an inalienable right of modern man which brooks no interference.' There have been numerous other recent challenges along these lines both from intellectuals generally and from those associated with the cause of workers. Recently, reformist scholars have established on Hainan Island another reform-minded think-tank called the China (Hainan) Institute for Reform and Development (*Zhongguo Hainan Gaige Fazhan Yanjiuyuan*).[11] This institute is known for its liberal attitude towards reform.

The writings of intellectuals that embrace universal standards and reject the key elements of China's official stance often share common ground with contemporary views evident in the debate in Hong Kong and the wider world. Several essays in this volume by Hong Kong and Western writers consider these arguments. These views may range from arguments concerning liberal theory, as discussed by Margaret Ng and Claude Lefort, to rigorous analysis of the merits of international and domestic legal processes, as discussed in the last part of this book by Christine Loh, Anna Wu, and myself. While the essays in this volume generally reflect on the struggles and difficulties of human rights in Asia, Claude Lefort's essay reflects on similar difficulties in the West.

The domestic Chinese debate is especially attentive to arguments about culture and the alleged unsuitability of human rights to Chinese soil. Both this essay and that of Eliza Lee point to the discursive avenues in contemporary human rights theory for engaging the culture-based challenge. The essays of Yu Haocheng and Zhu Feng reflect the course both the cultural and economic development arguments have taken, as well as the practical reality of human rights in contemporary China. Claude Lefort's essay shows that human rights produced no less dissension when they were introduced in the French Declaration of the Rights of Man as alien concepts in French society two hundred years ago. Lefort also sets the stage for considering external elements by introducing the roots of the universalist argument in the international human rights debate, of which the Chinese debate is just one subset. The international human rights debate has been an important factor in China's human rights development.

The External Challenge

The final weapon in China's formal official arsenal is its conception of sovereignty, which seriously resists outside interference. This was recently emphasized in the official white paper on Human Rights in China and in the Bangkok Declaration. The government sought to place human rights firmly in the domestic sphere by discouraging outside interference in its 'internal affairs'.

In addition to sovereignty, the white paper emphasized the importance of the 'right of subsistence' — the basic right to be fed and sheltered — over other rights. This right fits under the general category of social welfare rights (focusing on the economic and social well-being of citizens), emphasized by socialist and developing countries over the political or civil rights (relating to democracy, free speech, etc.) emphasized by capitalist developed countries. According to this view a country must have sovereignty to rule itself without outside interference and be able to meet the subsistence needs of its people before it can aspire to other human rights achievements.

The Chinese Government effectively carried these themes into the Bangkok Declaration, but failed to get them adopted at the United Nations World Conference on Human Rights in Vienna.[12] The Bangkok Declaration reflects Asia's official view on human rights, a view which is aggressively challenged by the numerous Asian NGOs which attended the meetings in Bangkok and Vienna.[13] At the Vienna meeting, the head of the Chinese delegation, Liu Huaqiu, articulated China's official views concerning international human rights, both with respect to culture and the other aspects noted above, as follows:

> The concept of human rights is a product of historical development. It is closely associated with specific social, political and economic conditions and the specific history, culture and values of a particular country. Different historical development stages have different human rights requirements .... Thus, one should not and cannot think the human rights standards and models of certain countries as the only proper ones and demand all other countries to comply with them. It is neither realistic nor workable to make international economic assistance or even international economic co-operation conditional on them.
> .... For the vast number of developing countries, to respect and protect human rights is first and foremost to ensure the full realization of the rights to subsistence and development. ...
> .... Nobody shall place his own rights and interests above those of the state and society, nor should he be allowed to impair those of others and the general public. This is a universal principle of all civilized societies. ...
> .... To wantonly accuse another country of abuse of human rights and impose the human rights criteria of one's own country or region on other countries or regions are tantamount to an infringement upon the sovereignty of other countries and interference in the latter's internal affairs, which could result in political instability and social unrest in other countries. ... State sovereignty is the basis for the realization of citizens' human rights. If the sovereignty of a state is not safeguarded, the human rights of its citizens are out of the question, like a castle in the air.[14]

Western governments, international and regional NGOs, and numerous scholars, including writers of several essays herein, have fostered a significant challenge to the above-noted sovereignty arguments in China's human rights policy. In her essay on the Vienna process, Christine Loh points out how the Chinese sovereignty arguments, also embodied in the Bangkok Declaration, were severely criticized by Chinese dissidents and Asian and international NGOs in Bangkok and in Vienna. In his essay, Yu Haocheng joins in this condemnation, offering a theoretical basis for such rejection. The argument for sovereignty as a base of resistance to international human rights obligations was also ultimately rejected in watered-down form by the Vienna Declaration and Programme of Action. The United Nations (UN) establishment of the office of the UN High Commissioner for Human Rights some six months later in December of 1993 further clarified this international resistance, though, as Christine Loh points out, the jury is still out on the success of this office and the adequacy of international support.

The challenge to China's theory of nearly absolute sovereignty began in the early twentieth century when the international treaty regime began to expand dramatically in a shrinking world. The realm of exclusive state control retreated as the inclusive order grew. At the same time, deep-rooted notions of popular sovereignty encouraged the trend to expand the regime of human rights and self-determination to better secure the exercise of popular will and meet common aspirations for human dignity. In her essay, Christine Loh describes the growing international human rights treaty regime and notes the several official international bodies charged with human rights enforcement.

Asia remains the weakest link in the international human rights regime as the only part of the world not covered by a regional human rights treaty. Several East and South-East Asian countries, including Burma, Cambodia, Vietnam, Indonesia, the Philippines, North Korea, and China, for example, have recently been severely criticized for their human rights records.

In this context the Bangkok Declaration may represent a form of progress. While the many hard-line Asian regimes and a few Asian democracies joined hands in arguing against complete application of universal standards and advanced various cultural and economic development arguments, they also acknowledged wide scope for universal standards and the processes of human rights. We should rightly fear that the cultural and developmental exceptions are taken more seriously than the affirmations of universal standards, given the human rights records of several of the governments involved.

Nevertheless, it is noteworthy that the Bangkok Declaration included an Asia-wide official affirmation of the Universal Declaration of Human Rights, stressed the importance of education and training in human rights, recognized the responsibility of states to promote human rights through appropriate infrastructure and legal mechanisms, emphasized the importance of guaranteeing human rights for various minority groups, underlined the need to take international measures to implement human rights, and acknowledged the importance of co-operation and dialogue with NGOs. While these and other commitments appear to be empty promises in many countries, on the present record, it is significant that these commitments be acknowledged. Implementation represents a challenge to Asia and the international community.

The pressure brought to bear on China by developed Western countries is another important aspect of the external dimension. In recently de-linking the United States' Most Favored Nation (MFN) trading status from China's human rights practices, the US administration seemed to question the use of continuing trade sanctions in periods of more stable relations. Indications are they will instead target trade-specific human rights issues, such as worker safety, protection of property rights, prison and child labour, and protection of women, in the future. At the same time, the administration has tried but failed to set up a bilateral Human Rights Commission. It now seems set to establish a US monitoring body and has encouraged voluntary operating principles for US companies.[15] The US and other countries have also sent numerous human rights delegations to China. China, however, has proven increasingly effective in using its growing economic power to deflect foreign governments' political pressure over its human rights record.

The more serious external pressure in the 1990s, barring dramatic developments, seems set to come from the international NGOs. These organizations, though severely strapped financially, have become increasingly effective in drawing attention to human rights violations, working with local pressure groups and activists, and identifying prisoners of conscience locked away in Chinese prisons. The most well-known of these groups include the Lawyers Committee for Human Rights and Asia Watch (which hosts a dissident pressure group called Human Rights in China) based in New York and Amnesty International based in London. Their efforts have frequently caused the Chinese and other governments to explain their human rights practices.

A Domestic Attempt to Legislate Rights

Given the strong emphasis that Chinese official policy and the Bangkok Declaration place on national sovereignty and non-interference, one could view it as a challenge to develop adequate domestic institutions to implement human rights and encourage a rich human rights discourse. Such development has not occurred. As discussed by Yu Haocheng and noted above, such institutions are virtually non-existent in China. Given the current underdevelopment of legal institutions, there is little prospect for significant improvement in the near future.

The essays on the Hong Kong Bill of Rights and on a proposed Human Rights and Equal Opportunities Commission for Hong Kong serve to illustrate the potential for success in an Asian community. Hong Kong has one of the more effective, if not the most effective, bills of rights in Asia. The Hong Kong Bill of Rights as discussed in my other essay is modeled almost verbatim on the International Covenant on Civil and Political Rights. The application of that covenant is assured under both the Sino-British Joint Declaration respecting Hong Kong and under China's Basic Law for the future Hong Kong Special Administrative Region.

The Hong Kong Bill of Rights embodies a common law system of judicial review in all the courts, what Mauro Cappelletti calls a 'decentralized (all courts have the power of review) incedenter (review may be sought incedental to any case, and not just by special certification) system'.[16] This has afforded a formal judicial avenue for human rights issues to be decided in an orderly and less politicized manner. Unfortunately, the extraordinary cost of litigation under Hong Kong's legal system, which is not very plaintiff-friendly, has discouraged civil claims. The vast majority of bill of rights claims have been in criminal cases.

In this context the proposal to set up a Human Rights and Equal Opportunities Commission, which Anna Wu discusses in her essay, was advanced. This seeks to fill in the gaps left by the Bill of Rights by offering a cost-effective and non-politicized avenue for human rights enforcement and oversight. It is interesting to note that, by initially emphasizing conciliation when disputes arise, this proposal seems to adhere to the expected standards of conflict resolution under allegedly less adversarial Asian social conditions.

The Hong Kong Bill of Rights and any Human Rights and Equal Opportunities Commission may, nevertheless, come to nought as the Chinese government has indicated that it will set aside both of these domestic human rights institutional arrangements if they are on the books in 1997 when China resumes sovereignty over Hong Kong. It is generally believed that this threat is the basis for the British Hong Kong Government's refusing to accept the legislative proposal for a Human Rights and Equal Opportunities Commission, and offering much more limited measures instead. One can only hope that governments that are committed in the Bangkok Declaration to developing human rights domestically in a way consistent with historical conditions will not inhibit the normal historical progression towards human rights development in a society for which they bear sovereign responsibility.

Conclusion

It is clear from China's official policy, as well as the Bangkok Declaration, that the Chinese government comes down firmly on the side of exclusivity and cultural relativism and against universal standards. One must ask whether these positions are at polar opposites and mutually exclusive. In other words, must one choose between cultural integrity and universal standards for the respect of human rights? In a discursive approach, universal standards can be the product of shared culture or cultural interaction.

On a local level this discourse can continue to have many local elements. In fact, under the inevitable onslaught of cultural change, open discussion may sometimes aid in the identification of those elements which can be preserved without undermining the fundamental commitment to emerging human rights values. It may simply be true in the present age that the number of universally accepted values is increasing as the level of interaction and human rights discourse increases.

Perhaps, as de Toqueville discovered in America, by the time we have formulated a response to emerging values or views to which our society is attracted we have already begun the process of assimilating these values.[17] When Samuel P. Huntington speaks of the clash of civilizations as defining our future world order, perhaps he underestimates the speed of value change and assimilation when such clashes occur.[18]

China, in formulating a response to what it argues are imperialistic pressures for universal human rights standards, appears to concede much more in its frequent justifications and in the Bangkok Declaration than it refutes. As the several other essays in this book reveal, Chinese scholars and, by their scholarly analysis, Chinese officials and society, have already assimilated far more of modern human rights values than either the government or the drafters of the Bangkok Declaration would care to admit.

If one looks at the quality of the human rights debate in Chinese society one is struck by the rich diversity of perspectives. This diversity reflects human rights values in the making. Debates about law and institutions are ultimately about values; these debates point to avenues for change. It is important to note that in the Bangkok Declaration Asian governments were formulating a response not only to a Western challenge but primarily to the challenge of their own people. This seems to be the primary reason for their response. As the recent US capitulation over the MFN debate reveals, Western power, whether it be military or economic, represents a much less serious challenge to Asian governments who would abuse human rights than the people of Asia themselves.

It is this challenge in China and Hong Kong that, in recent years, has produced the seemingly contradictory combination of both official resistance to the human rights challenge and official justification of policies in terms of that challenge. The latter includes a daily media blitz and a plethora of legislation (on legal process, prisoners' rights, equal rights for women and minorities, economic regulations, etc.), agreements over Hong Kong, reports, white papers, and international declarations and treaties. By the time the governments of the region are called upon to formulate such responses as are revealed in the Bangkok Declaration and the other policy pronouncements discussed above, they have already conceded far more than they would care to admit. This may not mean they are ready to capitulate. Especially in the short term, it may even mean that those who seek to retain power will redouble their efforts to silence their opposition, at the same time that their moral authority wanes.

The power of the ideas offered by Chinese and other intellectuals, both within and outside of China, offers the greatest challenge to those who would resist claims for greater adherance to universal standards of behaviour concerning human rights and the greatest hope for Chinese and Asian societies, as well as the world at large. Such ideas offer the hope of transforming political institutions and values, even as those in power appear to resist.

Notes

1. The Bangkok Declaration, Declaration of the Ministers and Representatives of Asian States, Bangkok, 29 March–2 April 1993. See Appendix. The meeting in Bangkok was the Asian preparatory meeting for the United Nations World Conference on Human Rights, held in Vienna between 14 and 25 June 1993. For discussion of the Vienna process and the Bangkok Declaration see the essay by Christine Loh.
2. See, e.g. Alexander M. Bickel, *The Least Dangerous Branch: The Supreme Court at the Bar of Politics*, 2nd edn., New Haven: Yale University Press, 1986; John H. Ely, *Democracy and Distrust: A Theory of Judicial Review*, Cambridge: Harvard University Press, 1980; Bruce A. Ackerman, *Social Justice in the Liberal State*, New Haven: Yale University Press, 1980; Myers McDougal, W. Michael Reisman, *International Law Essays: A Supplement to International Law in Contemporary Perspective*, Mineola, New York: The Foundation Press, 1981. For analysis of the critical perspective see the essay of Eliza Lee.
3. See Lee C. Bollinger, *The Tolerant Society: Freedom of Speech and Extremist Speech in America*, New York: Oxford University Press, 1986.
4. Owen M. Fiss, 'Two Constitutions,' *Yale Journal of International Law*, 11 (1986): 492.
5. R. Randle Edwards, Louis Henkin, Andrew J. Nathan, *Human Rights in Contemporary China*, New York: Columbia University Press, 1986.
6. Ann D. Jordan, 'Women's Rights in the People's Republic of China: Patriarchal Wine Poured from Socialist Bottles,' *Journal of Chinese Law*, 8 (1994): 1.
7. *Human Rights in China*, Beijing: Information Office of the State

Council (IOSC), 1991; *China's Reformed Criminals*, Beijing: IOSC, 1992; *Tibet's Sovereignty and Human Rights*, Beijing: IOSC, 1992.

8. Feng Zhu, *The Theory of Karl Marx on Human Rights Published in the German-French Yearbook (Lun 'De Fa Nian Jian' Shi Qi Ma Ke Si De Si Xiang)*, *Journal of Political Studies*, 3 (1992). The reference to the German-French Yearbook is to the two essays, 'Contribution to the Critique of Hegel's Philosophy of Right: Introduction' and 'On the Jewish Question' published in said yearbook in 1843.

9. Ta V. Tai, *The Vietnamese Tradition of Human Rights*, Berkeley: Institute of East Asian Studies, 1988.

10. 'Alarm at Challenge to Leaders,' *South China Morning Post*, 11 March 1994, p. 1.

11. 'Leadership Jostle Gives Think-tank Shot in Arm,' *South China Morning Post*, 6 June 1994, p. 9. In late February 1995, leading intellectuals also openly petitioned a session of the National People's Congress calling for control of official corruption, social justice, human rights, and democracy, '12 Intellectuals Petition China On Corruption', *New York Times*, 26 February 1995, p. A1; 'In Beijing Dissidents File New Petitions', *New York Times*, 28 February 1995, p. A8.

12. United Nations World Conference on Human Rights: Vienna Declaration and Programme of Action, Adopted 25 June 1993, 32 *I.L.M.* 1661 (1993).

13. *Our Voice, Bangkok NGO Declaration on Human Rights*, Reports of the Asia Pacific NGO Conference on Human Rights and NGOs' Statements to the Asia Regional Meeting (Bangkok: Asian Cultural Forum on Development, 1993). At the Bangkok meeting there were over 150 groups from Asia represented, plus another fifty Asian branches of broader international human rights groups.

14. Speech by Liu Huaqiu, Head of the Chinese Delegation at the World Conference on Human Rights (Vienna: Permanent Mission of the PRC to the United Nations in Vienna, 15 June 1993).

15. 'Goal Post Shift on Human Rights,' *South China Morning Post*, 7 June 1994, Business Post 6.

16. Mauro Cappelletti, *Judicial Review in the Contemporary World*, The Bobbs-Merrill Company, Inc., 1971.

17. Alexis de Tocqueville, *Democracy in America*, New York: Vintage Books, 1945.

18. Samuel P. Huntington, 'The Clash of Civilizations?' *Foreign Affairs*, 72 (3) (1993).

Part II
Classical Roots

Human Rights Today

Claude Lefort

The contemporary human rights debate in Asia and elsewhere has raised many questions regarding the nature and continuing vitality of human rights. This debate is rooted in much earlier discussions related to these questions. Recent social change in democratic countries, conflicts between democracy and totalitarianism, and attempts to find agreement on an international scale have displaced much of the original debate. However, in my view, not only has the prime conception of human rights not become obsolete, but we can now better evaluate its political import. I would like to make four points with respect to the definition and development of human rights.

First point. The notion of human rights still bears the mark of the unresolved issues raised by the 1789 French Declaration of the Rights of Man. This Declaration marked a turning point. Undoubtedly, it inherited a tradition rooted in the theories of natural law and social contract; it benefited from the recent American Declaration of Independence and the creation or transformation of legislation in the new states, which were themselves inspired by the seventeenth-century English Bill of Rights (the 1688 Bill was preceded by the 1623 Petition of Rights).

Yet, the French Declaration distinguished itself on the grounds of its systematic character and its explicit claim to universal meaning. It was to be severely criticized from several, even opposing, points of view. A conservative thinker, Joseph de Maistre, attached as he was to the French monarchy, considered the duties of people towards the nation to be in opposition to individual rights, which he felt would ruin the foundations of the social order. 'Freely slaves', he said, French subjects have been acting 'both voluntarily and necessarily. They do really what they wanted to do, but without deranging the general plans'. Of the Rights of Man he remarked ironically, 'I have seen, during my life, French, Italian, Russian, and other people. Moreover, I know, thanks to Montesquieu, that it is also allowed for one to be a Persian.

However, as to Man, I declare that I have never met him. If he exists, it is without my knowledge.'[1]

One of the most prominent liberal thinkers, Edmund Burke, claimed that the rights of English citizens were inherited and anchored in the thirteenth century's Magna Carta.[2] Separated from citizenship, rights no longer mean anything. On the other side, Marx made a radical critique of the Rights of Man in 'On the Jewish Question'.[3] Examining every article of the French Declaration, he stated that they were designed to disguise the new relations established in a bourgeois society, that is, to conceal the reign of private property under the veil of freedom. Both the notion of human nature and that of the independence of the individual, he believed, were to be rejected.

Those objections have not vanished. Now, we must ask ourselves if we can preserve human rights from the fiction of the nature of Man and if we can preserve individual freedom from the fiction of society as an association between individuals.

Second point. Let us observe that the rise of social and cultural rights, as a new category of human rights in the nineteenth century, and their multiplication in our time, have largely transformed the debate. On the one hand, it can be said that human rights, previously denounced as merely 'formal' by Marxism, have taken root in social reality, becoming more concrete. This remark encourages a relativistic view: human rights are said to be dependent on historical and social change.

On the other hand, many critics, attached to liberalism, have pointed out the risk of increasing the role of the State. New rights, they say, are no longer just confined to restricting the State. Henceforth, the function of human rights is to give satisfaction to social demands, once they have been admitted under the pressure of some category of people. Rights tend to become nothing more than credits. Consequently, the State is led to draw more and more important resources from civil society and to exercise an increasingly strict control upon the life of the citizens, who are expecting its intervention. The State becomes managerial as rights are transformed into socially recognized needs.

We must now ask whether the so-called social and cultural rights indicate progress in the conception of human rights

or whether, without necessarily agreeing with certain dem-
agogic critiques of the welfare state, we must distinguish these
'rights' from fundamental freedoms.

Third point. Human rights have played an increasingly
important role in international discussions. No doubt, the
1789 Declaration had given them a universal meaning. But
it was only after the First World War that a plan appeared,
in connection with such things as the League of Nations and
related domestic initiatives, to spread liberal principles everywhere. This simply failed. The turning point was marked by
the Charter of the United Nations which embodied social
and cultural rights to a large extent.

Those who initiated its Universal Declaration bore in mind,
of course, the new developments of rights in democratic countries. However, in my view, the creators were also guided by
the desire to craft a text suitable for the communist governments and their allies. Aware of the attraction of Marxist
ideology (perhaps even impressed by it), they searched for a
language capable of overcoming political opposition.

Without asking about the practical effects the Universal
Declaration has had, I observe that its text is ambiguous.
Each government can find the opportunity to accentuate one
particular right or another, give it priority, and thereby place
itself under the general banner of human rights. It can say,
in response to the reproach of violating individual freedoms
'we do have an appreciation of human rights of our own.'

Moreover, one should wonder whether what are called
'social rights' in communist countries correspond to what is
understood as such in democratic countries. In democratic
countries, we are faced with demands coming from the
people. In each case, we must decide if people who claim
'we have the right to' are referring to universal principles, or
whether they are expressing particular collective wishes, however respectable these wishes may be.

On the other hand, in totalitarian regimes, the government
must take measures to meet certain of the population's needs,
but its decisions are self-preserving: it may ignore any demand
which leaves its orbit. Power decides and bestows; it is always
arbitrary, and always selective. Individuals receive no more
than requisites disguised as rights, for they are treated as
dependents and not as citizens.

In any event, must we now distinguish between what

people consider as their rights, rights no government can alter, and state legislation or policy? To come back to the spirit of the Universal Declaration of the United Nations, the prime question is: can human rights be considered only as pre-political?

Fourth point. Movements for human rights, or spectacular individual protests in the name of them, appeared, in the 1970s, in countries subjected to totalitarian power or dictatorships, and they have shaken international public opinion. Such movements had been developing outside the political parties (where they still existed, of course) or ideological currents. They often proceeded without working out any political platform, and were frequently promoted with a view to avoiding frontal attack against the government. Everywhere — in Russia, China, and Eastern Europe, as well as in Brazil, Argentina, and Chile — people living under dictatorships used the same language.

From the characteristics of those movements and the protests of Eastern dissidents, certain observers have drawn the conclusion that human rights proved not to be political. Nonetheless, it is a remarkable fact that the human rights which stood in stark opposition to totalitarian or dictatorial governments in the late twentieth century were the same ones brought forth at the end of the eighteenth century. In spite of urgent social needs, the claims now and then were the guarantees of security, the protection against arbitrary arrests, prohibition of torture, and freedom of acting, speaking, meeting, and associating. So, is it not clear that those claims have a political significance, and that, while not aiming at political objectives, in the narrow sense of this word, they nevertheless lay down the principles of a political society?

Assessment

Now, I shall return briefly to the first question raised by the 1789 French Declaration. I do not deny, of course, that it was guided by the idea of natural rights which would reside within every individual. Nor am I am denying that political society was conceived as an association between independent individuals and its goal was the preservation of their rights.

Yet, how can we fail to see that the French Declaration promotes notions which are meaningful only if they are contrasted with those that governed the old monarchic order of
the *ancien régime?* This order was held to be both natural
and founded upon a definite social classification, by virtue
of which everyone should be fixed to his rank, at a determined distance from the others standing above or below him,
whereas power should appear as standing above the whole
society and possessing absolute legitimacy.

Significantly, the French Declaration begins with the proclamation of the end of any social distinction. What does
the notion of 'Man' mean, it was asked? In the first place,
we see that natural inequality is rejected. And immediately
the vision of an organically differentiated society, a society
conceived as a natural body, collapses. In consequence, the
image of a government claiming to be the head of such a
body and to possess full sovereignty is necessarily destroyed.
So, the third article states, 'the principle of all sovereignty
resides in the Nation.'

If we now examine those rights which seem to refer solely
to the individual, we find that they too have a political
import. That import, I concede, is not immediately clear for
readers who stick to the letter of the Declaration, but we
must also investigate the effects in social life of the exercise
of individual rights.

Marx always concentrated upon the form in which they
were established. He pursued every sign of naturalism and
individualism (egotism, as he called it) in order to assign it
an ideological function. Therefore Marx detected in the freedom of movement and the freedom of opinion for all, and
in the guarantees of security, no more than the establishment of a new model which enshrines the separation of
man from man. He thought rightly that naturalism and individualism were features characteristic of his time. But when
he dismissed the upheaval in social and political relations
connected with the bourgeois vision of the new rights, he
remained caught up in the ideological framework he claimed
to destroy.

Paradoxically, the most virulent critic of bourgeois ideology was trapped by it. He was convinced that it masked the
advent of a society shattered into private interests, coinciding
with the arrival of a state designed to embody a fictitious

sovereignty. In fact, human rights are not, as he said, a veil. Far from concealing the dissolution of the social bonds which would make everyone a monad, human rights both testified to a new network of human relations and brought them into existence.

Indeed, in the French Declaration the right of freedom of movement enshrines the lifting of prohibitions characteristic of the *ancien régime*. Everyone would now have the right to settle where they wish, to travel as they wish across the territory of the nation, to enter places which were previously the preserve of privileged categories, to embark upon careers for which they believe they are qualified.

The freedom of opinion does not transform opinion into private property and it is not modeled on the ownership of material goods. According to the text of the French Declaration, 'the free communication of opinions and thoughts is one of the most precious rights of man; every citizen may therefore speak, write and freely print, unless what he does constitutes an abuse of that liberty in the particular cases laid down by law. . . .' Consider that the fact of speaking, writing, or printing, goes along with the fact of listening to or reading and transmitting; that, not only does each one possess the same rights, but each one is related to the others through the exercise of those rights; that circulation of opinions develops and ensures a sort of irrigation of the social fabric. Moreover, opinions and thoughts, once recognized, can be transformed in interaction with one another. So, a symbolic space comes into being, without definite frontiers and outside of political authority. Lastly, the guarantees of security, in which Marx found only the most sordid expression of civil society — a 'concept of police' designed to protect bourgeois property — teach us that justice, just as the faculty of thinking and knowing, has been separated from power. Justice is (theoretically) governed by its own principles and, by protecting the individual from arbitrariness, makes him a symbol of the freedom which founds the social links.

Did human rights — such as they were conceived of at the end of the eighteenth century — mark only an episode within European history? They certainly have to be analysed against a specific background. But, however striking are the features of the great European societies under the *ancien régime*, in contrast with Chinese, Indian, or even Russian societies, we observe that the former were partly governed by representations operating in all large forms of society, although other beliefs, such as the idea of natural hierarchy, society as a natural body, social relations as imprinted in universal order, and individuals as parts of a whole (family, lordship, kingdom, or empire) also influenced the governments of the late eighteenth century. By breaking with the principles which guided the old European order, the philosophy of human rights shook the bases of any régime hitherto existing.

This philosophy brought to light a fundamental opposition which concerns every country in the world. In fact, everywhere, at different times, the representations I have just mentioned have been undermined, and the same alternatives encountered: either admitting the model of a plural, conflicting society open to change, in which, as de Tocqueville said, one tries to use freedom itself to fight against the excesses of freedom, or obstinately denying plurality, prohibiting any initiative which escapes the control of power, accrediting the fantasy of the people-as-one through new means of coercion. Many countries have hesitated, searching for a compromise. Communism, for its part, has resolutely involved itself in the second one; it has, apparently in vain, attempted to realize, under the cover of a revolution against capitalism, an anti-democratic revolution, designed to bar the way of human rights.

Conclusion

I offer three remarks to conclude:

First, concerning the distinction between human rights and social and cultural rights, it seems to me that the former constitute the fabric of democracy; the latter, at best, are woven into this fabric. Far from rendering human rights more concrete, their multiplication risks obscuring the *sense of rights*.

Second, concerning the new international dimension of rights, the most important task, in my view, is to insist upon the rights of the minorities within every nation and the minorities within that minority. It has become clear that the right of the people to be master of themselves has too often been used in order to disguise the political or cultural domination of a majority over an ethnic minority.

Lastly, as for the objections against a view of the universal value of human rights which would ignore the variety of cultures, one should observe that human rights are always applied to societies that are differently modeled by their historical inheritance, their customs, and beliefs. Often, cultural traditions can only survive if protected through the freedom of opinion (including, of course, religious opinions). On the other hand, culture is threatened by regimes which try to utilize some corrupt currents of tradition in order to reinforce their control over each domain of social life.

In fact, the French Declaration does not teach what Man is, or what human society must be. The objection that Man is undefined, in a sense, is right. However, it does not mean that Man is an abstraction. It rather means that he is recognized as indeterminably bound to remain in quest of himself — unless he prefers servitude.

Notes

1. Joseph de Maistre, 'Considerations on France', in *The Works of Joseph de Maistre*, translated by Jack Lively, New York: Schocken Books, 1971, p. 80.
2. Edmund Burke, *Reflections on the Revolution in France*, New York: Doubleday Anchor Books, 1973, p. 43.
3. Karl Marx, 'On the Jewish Question', in Robert C. Tucker (ed.), *The Marx-Engels Reader*, New York: W. W. Norton & Co., 1972, p. 24.

Relating Human Rights To Chinese Culture: The Four Paths of the Confucian Analects and the Four Principles of a New Theory of Benevolence

Du Gangjian and Song Gang

The 'theory of benevolence' (*ren xue*) is of great and universal significance in the *Confucian Analects* (hereinafter '*Analects*') and the extended Confucian tradition in Chinese culture. This traditional benevolence theory has traveled a tortuous and difficult path in the past millenia, coming almost to its end several times. During this period, although many Confucian scholars tried to resolve and explain the principles of the benevolence theory, they generally failed to keep it contemporary and failed to integrate it with world trends of civilization.

This essay seeks to render the theory of benevolence relevant to modern times by relating it to four contemporary principles. These four principles we have termed the ideologies of human rights (*ren quan zhu yi*), tolerance (*kuan rong zhu yi*), resistance (*di kang zhu yi*), and neo-constitutionalism (*xin xian zheng zhu yi*). Together these comprise what we will call a 'new benevolence theory'. They reflect our attempt to clarify key elements of the modern debate on human rights in China. This framework also structures the contemporary human rights debate in a way that facilitates comparison with classical Confucian theory.

These principles are important instruments in understanding the adaptability of human rights concepts to contemporary Chinese society. The classical components of the benevolence theory in the *Analects* include the paths of benevolence (*ren dao*), tolerance (*shu dao*), justice (*yi dao*), and government (*zheng dao*). One may say that these are the four fundamental principles of the classical Confucian benevolence theory, while the ideology of human rights, the ideology of tolerance, resistance, and neo-constitutionalism are the four fundamental principles of what we call the new benevolence theory.

It is important to consider the relationship between the classical theory of benevolence in the *Analects* and these four modern principles, as these principles may be said to animate the modern projects of human rights and constitutional government in China. Through this avenue we may consider the compatibility of classical Chinese Confucian culture and modern principles of human rights. This may assist us to develop a contemporary theory of human rights for Chinese society. Without advocating a completely Western form of democracy, we believe there is ample room within the traditional dictates of Chinese culture for a form of constitutional government which embodies a strong commitment to modern human rights values.

Our objective here is simply to argue that the modern concept of human rights is not alien to Chinese soil. This resists the argument that there is a cultural impediment to developing human rights in Chinese society. In order to accomplish our objective, this essay will concentrate primarily on identifying the elements in classical Confucian thought that bear comparison to modern principles of human rights, as these elements are framed in our new benevolence theory. We hope that this will assist the task of evaluating the cultural claims discussed throughout the present volume.

The Path of Benevolence in the Analects and the Modern Ideology of Human Rights

We use the term human rights ideology to refer to the ideological trend in modern China to seek an overall and thorough fulfilment of human rights. This trend was historically related to the emergence of socialism.[1] Human rights ideology, as a systematic school, is still in its infancy, being largely a characterization we employ to describe the leading edge of the recent intellectual debate and its embrace in the popular movements of the late 1980s.

The origins of this modern concept of human rights ideology in China include different ideological trends of human rights in Western history, especially those trends of socialist human rights, as well as those ideas and values related to the development of human rights in traditional Chinese culture. The latter include such concepts from Confucianism as benevolence (*ren dao*), humanism (*ren ben zhu yi*), individualism (*ge ren zhu yi*), and activism (*zuo wei zhu yi*).

One of the important features of human rights ideology is to regard the maintenance of personality and human dignity as the fundamental aim in building up the political and legal community. A series of concepts, such as personality, dignity, human nature, humanity, rationality, conscience, and benevolence, constitute the important cornerstones of contemporary human rights theory.[2] Although the term 'human rights' did not appear in the *Analects*, many of the values advocated therein are quite similar to those of this contemporary human rights ideology. They provided rich material for modern Chinese development of human rights theory.

Moreover, the classical path of benevolence may be quite useful in contemporary efforts to expound the notion of human rights ideology. The fundamental nature of contemporary human rights ideology can be said to be based upon benevolence in the maintenance of personal dignity. The *Analects* mention the word 'benevolence' 109 times. The following basic principles of the classical benevolence path are worthy of discussion.

The original meaning of benevolence was to 'love all men'. Although there were several explanations of this statement's implications in the *Analects*, what was most important was to love the people. Fanchi, a discip'e of Confucius, asked about benevolence. Confucius said, 'It is to love all men.'[3] 'A man should overflow in love to all, and cultivate the friendship of the good.'[4] He suggested that to love the people is to treat all people, not just one's family, as the objects of love. 'All within the four seas will be his brothers.'[5] Nevertheless, the spirit of loving all needs to start from loving one's own family members. This point includes the idea that 'filial piety and fraternal submission are the roots of all benevolent actions.'[6]

To love the people one needs to treat people in a humane way and respect them. Therefore, 'reverence' (*gong*) and 'respect' (*jing*) should become the code of conduct. Confucius said, 'The filial piety of nowadays means the support of one's parents. But dogs and horses likewise are able to do something in the way of support, but without reverence; what is it that distinguishes the one support given from the other?'[7]

Those who are not reverent, respectful, and filial will never be full of loving spirit. Respecting the personal dignity of others, however, does not mean losing one's own personal dignity. The benevolent spirit of filial piety and fraternal submission advocated in the *Analects* was often distorted to mean the absence of personal dignity. This runs counter to the benevolent thought in the *Analects*.

Benevolence is essential and propriety is practical (ren wei ti, li wei yong). Benevolence, as the source of all ethics, needs to be reflected in the conduct of rites (*li*). The notion of propriety, including filial piety, fraternal submission, reverence, respect, confidence (*xin*), benign behaviour (*wen*), uprightness (*liang*), temperateness (*jian*), modesty (*qian*), and tolerance (*rang*), is important because it reflects the benevolent spirit. As to their priority, benevolence is first and propriety is second. Benevolence is the soul of propriety and propriety is the practice of benevolence. To argue that one should 'deny self and return to propriety' and that 'filial piety and fraternal submission is the root of benevolence' is to talk about the process of fulfilling benevolence. The relationship between benevolence and propriety should not be reversed. If one fails to understand this one will carry on unchecked and fail to avoid those rites which are illegal and opposite to benevolence in current social life.

It is everyone's duty to promote benevolence in the world. The *Analects* advocated that everyone should make great efforts to seek benevolence, to regard it as his duty, and to become virtuous. To consider benevolence as a lifelong target embodied religious love toward human beings and praise of the human subject's nature. 'If the will be set on virtue, there will be no practice of wickedness.'[8] Activism was one of the important principles in the *Analects*. 'It is only the (truly) virtuous man, who can love or who can hate others.'[9] Yet it was much easier to be virtuous than to take action to promote virtue. The virtuous man and the benevolent actor are two different targets on two different levels. Both reflect the activist spirit.

Benevolence depends upon individuals. The *Analects* paid close attention not only to the human subject's nature, but to his personality. It can be said that human individualism (*ge ren ben wei zhu yi*) was another principle of the benevolent path. Each person has his own capacity to accomplish benevolence.

A virtuous man emerges in the process of dealing with re-lations among people so that selfness (*zi wo*) becomes the centre of relations. The *Analects* confirmed the inherent lib-erty of humans and encouraged people to try to understand this aspect. Self-reliance brings human initiatives and de-cisiveness to light, embodying the combination of activist and individualist principles. The benevolent path regarded‛ the self as the centre of internal and external co-ordination. A person improves the external environment in order to improve himself.

The four points mentioned above show that the notion of benevolence in the *Analects* affords a theoretical foundation and fertile soil for human rights ideology. Both notions emphasize human dignity, the significance of human nature, human subjectivity (*ren de ben ti xing*), a dynamic human role, and human independence and freedom. This contrasts with the current human rights nihilism in China. Considering this historically rooted notion of benevolence will help us to overcome the nihilist argument that human rights have no place in China and will help us to improve the spirit of socialist human right ideology.[10]

The Path of Tolerance and the Modern Ideology of Tolerance

The term 'ideology of tolerance' has roots in the Western philosophical theory of relativism propounded by the German jurist Gustav Radbruch. The fundamental spirit of the juristic-philosophical theory of relativism was tolerance. Gustav Radbruch characterized his theory as a theory of tolerance. The universal rise of that theory after the Second World War indicated an international juristic community given to deep introspection concerning the outrages of Nazism and Fascism. This juristic theory has had a significant effect upon the development of legal culture and social-economic reforms in modern East Asia.

The *Analects* reveal much deeper Asian roots for the notion of tolerance. Although the notion of the path of tolerance in the *Analects* is classical, it has important theoretical significance for the development of a modern theory of tol-erance. The tolerance path, which was subsumed under the

classical benevolence path, was an important part of benevolence theory in the *Analects*. It was also the main form
and category of tolerance theory in ancient China. These
paths sought both tolerance and benevolence at the same
time. Confucius said, 'Love is to hope others live well, hating is to hope others die soon. With such meaning, you will
be puzzled by both wanting love and hating.'[11]

Tolerance was therefore the logical desire of the spirit of
benevolence. 'The morality of a superior man is to treat everybody kindly and tolerantly.'[12] When one of his students asked
if there was one word which might serve as a rule of practice for all one's life, Confucius answered, 'Tolerance is just
such a word! Do not do unto others what you would not
like others to do unto you.'[13]

The path of tolerance also stressed that one should not
force others to do what they are reluctant to do. This idea
was based upon a deep insight into humanity. The tolerance
path particularly emphasized not harming others. This same
idea had an important influence on some French advocates
of the Enlightenment, such as Voltaire and Maximilien Robe-
spierre, and on the French Declaration of the Rights of Man
(1789) and later the Universal Declaration of Human Rights
(1948). Article 4 of the Rights of Man regarded freedom as
the right to do anything that did not bring harm to others,
while some of the Universal Declaration's articles, banning
slavery and forced labour, embodied the same spirit of
tolerance.

Although the idea, 'do not do unto others what you would
not like others to do unto you' might be applied as a general principle of morality (as with the 'golden rule' in the
West), it was mainly directed against rulers and stressed that
they should not force their subjects to do what the subjects
were reluctant to do. It is quite necessary to seek the tolerant spirit simply because many rulers are neither tolerant nor
benevolent. The combination of preventing evils and seeking tolerance formed the fundamental content of the tolerance path.

But we must not ignore the element of generosity in the
tolerance path. Zi Xia said, 'We should tolerate good and virtuous people, and refuse to tolerate the less able and less virtuous.' Zi Zhang, a student of Confucius said, 'A gentleman
respects the sage and tolerates the multitude; he praises good

people and feels pity or sympathy for people who are not so able and virtuous. If I am an able and virtuous person, I shall tolerate everybody.'[14] Confucius pointed out, 'To be able to practise five things everywhere under heaven constitutes perfect virtue: gravity, generosity of soul, tolerance, earnestness, and kindness.'[15] It is clear that 'generosity' and 'tolerance' were a very important part of the tolerance path in the *Analects*.

In addition to 'generosity' (*kuan*), 'tolerance' (*rong*), 'loyalty' (*zhong*), and 'endurance' (*ren*), the notions of 'harmony' (*he*), independence of 'speech' (*yan*), and 'academics' (*xue*) are also parts of the tolerance path in the *Analects*. Harmony provides the foundation and the achievement of the tolerance spirit in the *Analects*. 'The function of rites is to insist on harmony as best.'[16] The original meaning of harmony was to seek a peaceful environment even when there is no agreement (*tong*). 'The superior man is affable, but not adulatory; the mean man is adulatory, but not affable.'[17] It is inevitable that there are always differences in peoples' minds. It was very significant that the *Analects* sought harmony but not identicalness. The stability of a society could not depend upon force to get unanimity but could only depend upon the idea that 'when the people keep their several places, there will be no poverty; when harmony prevails, there will be no scarcity; and when there is such a contented repose, there will be no rebellion.'[18] Protection of personality and diversity, allowing their existence and development, are the preconditions for a society to develop peacefully.

The path of tolerance also included a sort of freedom of speech and academics. According to the *Analects*, everybody has his own words to say and the independence of speech should be protected. 'The superior man does not promote a man simply on account of his words, nor does he put aside good words because of the man.'[19] 'The virtuous will be sure to speak correctly, but those whose speech is good may not always be virtuous.'[20] Here the distinction between one's character and one's speech was stressed. Confucius sought to distinguish speech from action. He said, 'At first, my way with men was to hear their words, and give them credit for their conduct. Now my way is to hear their words, and look at their conduct.'[21] Seriously to distinguish speech from action is an important condition legally to protect the freedom of speech. The *Analects* advocated that speech was a pre-condition to trust a person. 'If you do not know a person's speech, you can not understand him.'[22]

The freedom of speech advocated in the *Analects* included: 'expression' (*fang yan*), 'careful speech' (*sheng yan*), and 'silence' (*wu yan*). According to the *Analects*, 'It may be said of Yu-chung and I-yi, that, while they hid themselves in their seclusion, they gave a license to their words; but, in their persons, they succeeded in preserving their purity, and, in their retirement, they acted according to the exigency of the times.'[23] The notion of 'expression', the act of speaking out, is an important part of the freedom of speech. The idea of 'careful speech' relates to the self-restriction of expression without any external pressure. Confucius said, 'To hear much with doubt, and to be prudent of speaking of what you hear, you will have little anxiety. To hear much without doubt and to be prudent of doing what you hear, you will have little regret. Then you will be happy with little anxiety and little regret.'[24] 'Expression' aimed mainly at commenting upon and criticizing the government and its policies, while the notion of 'careful speech' was mainly to warn rulers not to make arbitrary decisions or issue orders randomly; because 'a single sentence can ruin a country' (*yi yan sang ban*).

Meanwhile, people should be allowed not only to express themselves freely but also to keep silent. The freedom of silence was an important aspect of freedom of speech and thinking. Confucius said: 'Does heaven speak? The four seasons pursue their courses, and all things are continually being produced, but does heaven say anything?'[25] Freedom of silence is a natural right which even heaven demands.

It is note worthy that the freedom of speech advocated by Confucius referred mainly to the right to criticize government and to be a dissident. Confucius once expressed appreciation of Zichan's position (he was the emperor of Zhengguo State). When some people of Zhengguo gathered in the schools to criticize the government, some ministers suggested closing those schools. But Zichan refused and argued passionately that they should allow 'comments on the merits and defects of government'. He felt that leaders should listen to criticism and felt that honesty and kindness would reduce criticism; arbitrariness could not prevent criticism. After hearing his arguments, Confucius sang his praise. As a matter of fact, Confucius regarded making personal suggestions to rulers and commenting on and criticizing governments and their policies to be his personal responsibility. He stated angrily that 'a tyranny is just like a tiger' (*ke zheng meng yu hu*).

Judging by his speech and actions, Confucius was, to a large extent, a dissident. He not only advocated comments on and criticisms of government, he also advised rulers on how properly to treat criticism and different ideas. He urged them 'to correct the mistakes they made; to be careful, even if they had not made mistakes' (*you ze gai zhi, wu ze jia mian*). Rulers should have a tolerant and respectful attitude towards different ideas and criticisms. Repression, exclusion, and suppression of dissidents and their ideas reflects despotism and ruthless tyranny. Confucius said: 'When good government prevails in a State, language may be lofty and bold, and actions the same. When bad government prevails, the actions may be lofty and bold, but the language may be with some reserve.'[26] Such 'reserve' results from repressing speech and reflects a bad regime. The final outcome of repressing speech will be the a regime's collapse.

The path of tolerance in the *Analects* advocated not only freedom of speech, but a tolerant attitude toward academics (*jiang xue*). People were urged 'to learn so as to accomplish one's works and reach to the utmost of one's principles' (*xue yi cheng ren, xue yi zhi dao*). Learning was one of the very important theoretical categories in the *Analects* and the key to knowledge and tolerance. As mentioned above, that Confucius supported Zichan not ruining the schools, indicated that learning, or the freedom to learn, was undoubtedly an important element of the path of tolerance. Academic discourse should, of course, include comments on, and judgments about, governmental policies. Confucius pointed out, 'Neglect of godliness, study without understanding, failure to act according to what I believe to be right, and the inability to change bad habits, these are the things which cause me constant solicitude.'[27] To cultivate morality, to study, and to abandon evil were related to each other. Without academic freedom we are inevitably not able to distinguish good from evil; and it is difficult to correct a tyranny.

Besides advocating freedom of speech and discourse, the path of tolerance advocated that we forgive others' past misdeeds and 'pardon small defects' (*she xiao guo*). Confucius said, 'It is useless to speak of a thing that is done; to change a course that is begun; or to blame what is past and gone.'[28] 'Employ first the services of your various officers and raise to office men of virtue and talents.'[29] Among the seventy-two students of Confucius, Yanhui was the one who treated others with tolerance and behaved earnestly, 'never venting his anger on others and never repeating a fault'.[30] It is very helpful to overcome the emotions of sadness and hatred if one is taught through virtues such as loyalty, tolerance, warmth, and modesty. Then one might reach the heights of the path of tolerance.

The above principles are also the fundamental contents of the ideology of tolerance advocated by the authors of this essay. In applying the path of tolerance in today's China, it is necessary to advocate freedom of thinking and speech based upon the principle of seeking common points and allowing differences. The so-called modern ideology of tolerance emphasizes, first of all, the need to tolerate different ideas, especially those of dissidents. It is disingenuous to seek refuge for suppression in Chinese culture, in disregard of the tolerance path. The attitude taken by Confucius shows that freedom of speech is fundamental to the path of tolerance. By this reasoning it is very consistent with traditional Chinese culture to put freedom of speech foremost among human rights in contemporary China. Without the freedom of speech, people's minds cannot be emancipated. The spirit of the modern ideology of tolerance inherited from the concept of tolerance put forth in the *Analects* should be developed further and combined with contemporary needs of reform, opening to the outside world and emancipating the mind.

The Path of Justice and the Modern Principle of Resistance

We use the term resistance to describe the modern theoretical trend to advocate and expound the right to resist authority. Since the French Declaration of the Rights of Man (1789) treated the right to resist oppression as a fundamental right, the idea of the right of resistance has been a constant theme in the development of human rights. Especially since the Second World War and the experience of fascist rule, the right to resist corrupt rule and tyranny has been treated as a fundamental human right and incorporated in the constitutions of many countries. More and more political scientists and legal scholars have made efforts to expound and study the significance of the right to resist and have organized resistant movements.[31]

The notion of resistance in China is rooted in the Qin Dynasty writings of Confucius and Mencius (Mengzi). Many modern scholars who studied the ideological history of the right to resist thought that it was rooted in the West. Now they have gradually come to recognize that this concept also has Eastern roots.[32]

The path of justice discussed in the *Analects* introduced the classical notion of resistance. In the *Analects*, 'justice' (*yi*) is not less important than 'benevolence' (*ren*). Both justice and benevolence have higher authority than written law. Both were the highest principles of ethics insisted upon by people with lofty ideals. Confucius said, 'A wise man in his judgement of the world has no predilections nor prejudices; he is on the side of right.'[33]

In the *Analects*, as a principle of conduct to measure interpersonal relations, justice shared the same importance with rites (*li*). Confucius said, 'When agreements are made according to what is right, what is spoken can be made good. When respect is shown according to what is proper, one keeps far from shame and disgrace.'[34] And he also said to Zichan, 'There are four characteristics of a wise man: in his own conduct, he is humble; in serving his superiors, he is respectful; in nourishing the people, he is kind; in ordering the people, he is just.'[35]

In terms of modern legal culture, among the four paths, the theoretical significance of the path of justice is especially noteworthy. Justice is not only a general principle of ethics but more importantly a code of political behaviour. Justice is related closely to regulating the behaviour and conditions of the common people. The paths of justice, benevolence, and tolerance all provide guidance for political leaders.

The relationship between justice and benevolence was embodied in the notion of 'ethics' (*de*). The ethic of kindness was primary to the notion of justice. 'To seek justice' is just 'to respect kindness' (*tu yi jiu shi chong de*). Zi Zhang asked how virtue was to be exalted, and delusions discovered. Confucius said, 'Hold faithfulness and sincerity as

first principles, and be moving continually to what is right
— this is the way to exalt one's virtue. If you love a man
you wish him to live; if you hate him you may wish him to
die. Having wished him to live, if you also wish him to die,
this is a case of delusion'.[36]

To esteem benevolence was the original intention of justice; to seek justice and be helpful was also a noble ethic.
'To see justice' as 'esteeming ethics' was related to 'interests'
(*li*). Answering Fanchi's question about esteeming ethics',
Confucius said, 'If doing what is to be done be made the
first business, and success a secondary consideration, is not
this the way to exalt virtue?'[37]

It was the principle of 'esteeming ethics' that made justice
more important than interests. When the *Analects* talked
about justice, it was often related to interests. That justice
was prior to interests was a main feature of the path of justice in the *Analects*. Confucius said, 'The mind of the superior man is conversant with righteousness; the mind of the
mean man is conversant with gain.'[38] This was the difference
between a benevolent person and a money-worshipping vil-
lain. In respect of ideals, justice and interests were different
levels of values. As Confucius pointed out, 'Do not make
haste. Do not seek small profit. The more haste, the less
speed. He who seeks small profit succeeds in no major
principles.'[39]

Yet Confucius was not against interests: he advocated seeking interests, but insisted on adherence to the principles of
the path of justice. The principles of 'thinking of righteousness in the view of gain' (*jian li si yi*) and of 'taking when
it is consistent with righteousness to do so' (*yi ran hou qu*)
were the important preconditions.

There are nine things to consider before a monarch takes
an action. Confucius said, 'The superior man in everything
considers righteousness to be essential. He performs it according to the rules of propriety. He brings it forth in humility.
He completes it with sincerity'.[40] Regarding justice as a principle and refusing profits without justice were the real meanings of the Confucian justice path. 'The object of the superior
man is truth. Food is not his object' (*jun zi mou dao bu mou
shi*). 'The superior man is anxious lest he should not get
truth; he is not anxious lest poverty should come upon him'
(*jun zi you dao bu you pin*). It was the aim of people with

lofty ideals to seek justice. 'Riches and honours are what men desire. If they cannot be obtained in the proper way, they should not be held. Poverty and meanness are what men dislike. If they cannot be avoided in the proper way, they should not be avoided.'[41] It is no doubt that some principles of the justice path can be of importance in guiding economic and political conduct in a modern market economy.

The Confucian idea of the justice path aimed mainly at political behaviour. Seeking justice was to overcome injustice in public life. The *Analects* defined the standard for both justice and valour (*shang yi shang yong de biao zhun*). They stated, 'The superior man holds righteousness to be of highest importance. A man in a superior situation, having valour without righteousness, will be guilty of insubordination; inferior people having valour without righteousness, will be prone to commit robbery'.[42] Also according to Confucius, 'The wise are free from perplexities; the virtuous from anxieties; the bold from fear.'[43] Braveness must be based on benevolence. 'Men of principle are sure to be bold, but those who are bold may not always be men of principle.'[44]

The idea of combining braveness with justice in the *Analects* is the theoretical foundation for the idea of resistance. The argument of justice as a principle and justice as priority was to advocate the brave spirit of resisting injustice. Starting from the principle of the justice path, the concept of resistance was embodied in the following aspects.

First, one must be ready to take up the cudgels for a just cause. 'One who hesitates to do what is right is not brave.'[45] In order for gallantry to rise to the occasion, it needs the 'firm' (*gang*), 'outspoken' (*zhi*), and 'enduring' (*yi*) spirit. 'The man of distinction is solid and straightforward, and loves righteousness.'[46] 'To pursue the path of straightforwardness' (*zhi dao er xing*) was the main spirit of the justice path. If one says that the main features of the tolerance path were 'mildness', 'gentleness', and 'tolerance' (*wen, gong, rang*), then one may note that the comparable characteristics of the justice path were 'uprightness', 'outspokenness', and 'strength'. The outspoken spirit was to be bold, to insist on different ideas and to criticize government. 'Truly straightforward was the historiographer You. When good government prevailed in his State, he was like an arrow. When bad government prevailed, he was like an arrow'.[47]

Second, 'Do not support injustice and do not wait upon a non-benevolent monarch.' (*bu shi wu yi, yi dao shi jun*) The *Analects* advocated refusal to provide services to non-benevolent rulers and refusal to co-operate with them. 'As to the failure of right principles to make progress, a superior man is aware of that.'[48] To serve a monarch in accordance with the justice path was fundamental to the duty to co-operate with rulers. Confucius said, 'One serves his prince according to what is right, and when he finds he cannot do so, he retires.'[49] Morality was required in dealing with monarchs.

Third, keep a distance from tyranny and despots. 'When good government prevails in his state, a wise man is to be found in office. When bad government prevails, he can roll his principles up, and keep them in his breast.'[50] When one lives in any state, he should take up service with the most worthy among its great officers, and make friends of the most virtuous among its scholars. People with lofty ideals should choose right places with justice to live, should be far away from a state of despotic rule and go for shelter to a state of benevolent rule. 'The superior man thinks of virtue; the small man thinks of comfort.'[51] The freedom to choose a right place to live embodied the argument for freedom to go abroad and settle down. The modern advocacy of freedom of movement has a counterpart in the ancient Confucian notion of freedom to move because of dissatisfaction with government. Similarly Socrates argued that citizens should be allowed by law to leave a state because of their dissatisfaction with the government and law. However, if citizens were willing to stay, it was equal to giving tacit consent to the government and law, so that they were bound to obey all the regulations in that state. Patriotism (*yu zhong*) with benighted loyalty is out of tune with the justice path, which stressed the need to seek justice in the world but not to keep one's eyes on only one state.

Fourth, disobey the monarch's orders and resist injustice. It might have been said that the second and third points still belonged to negative resistance, but the practice of disobeying a monarch's orders and resisting injustice introduced a stage of positive resistance. While talking about instructions of political rulers, Confucius indicated that people should take a resistant attitude toward and measures against decrees issued by those non-benevolent rulers. 'If they are not good, and no one opposes them, may there not be expected from this the ruin of the country?'[52] 'If a minister cannot rectify himself, what has he to do with rectifying others?'[53] As for those despotic actions of 'ill-treating subjects' (*nue min*), 'killing subjects with maltreatment' (*bao min*), and 'persecuting subjects' (*can min*), Confucius thought that people could not be blamed for resisting the regime. He said, 'To put the people to death without having instructed them — this is called cruelty. To require from them, suddenly, the full scale of work, without having given them warning — this is called oppression. To issue orders as if without urgency, at first, and, when the time comes, to insist on them with severity — this is called injury.'[54] Confucius attacked such kinds of despotic actions angrily and tried to expound the argument that there was no blame upon people if they opposed despotic rule. This is the spirit of resistance.

Finally, the resistance concept of the justice path was fundamentally limited to the realm of non-violent resistance and conscientious objection. According to Confucius, 'Men of true ideal and goodwill do not do any harm to humanity and justice when alive and cherish the ambition of dying for a just cause.'[55] Although the *Analects* expressed concern about tyranny and despotism, it did not support the use of violence to punish despots. However, the argument in the *Analects* against tyranny and despotism was taken up by Mencius (*Mengzi*). Mencius later suggested using violence to resist autocrats. From non-violent resistance to violent resistance, Confucian thought developed in a radical direction. The moral spirit of sacrificing oneself for a just cause and laying down one's life for justice had a significant influence on China's history.

In terms of the modern theory of resistance, there are many elements in the justice path of the *Analects* worthy of further consideration and development. The non-violent trend in the *Analects* is especially worthy of consideration in modern civilized society. For thousands of years the Chinese solved serious social problems through violence. Under the guidance of violence, rational and peaceful forces did not prevail. As a result, rulers endlessly used violence as an antidote to violence. The long-term historical lessons and experiments have made clear to the world that violence stems from ignorance and backwardness; non-violence will guide humans toward a better civilization. After the Second World War, more and more nation-states struggling against wide-scale violence have encouraged and protected non-violent resistance in order to calm down popular discontent, relax contradictions and avoid serious confrontation.

The Government Path of the Analects and Neo-Constitutionalism

'Neo-constitutionalism' is the name given to the constitutional theory put forward by the authors of this essay. According to the 'government path' the structure of political administration in a state must be divided into two components: the ruler and the ruled. Confucianism never held that the people as a whole could be the masters, engaged directly in political administration. Confucianism was concerned with elite politics. Modern democracy is therefore somewhat alien to Chinese soil.

The Confucian theory in this regard finds resonance in modern Marxism. Marxist theory urges that the state is a tool of the ruling classes. Such domination will end as real democracy (direct democracy or peoples' autonomy) comes. Democratic government, such as that put forward by Aristotle for the city-states of ancient Greece, is impossible to realize under the conditions of modern nation-states, especially in such a large country as China. The fundamental principal of a democratic system is self-rule by the people. But under Marxism such autonomy can only realized after the withering away of the state. Therefore, even under Marxism the Confucian theory of the government path still has theoretical significance.

The neo-constitutionalism we advocate for China regards the protection and achievement of human rights as the object of constitutional government. Constitutionalism is different from democratic politics. The present constitutionalism in modern China ultimately seeks democracy but neglects the importance of protecting liberty and human rights. Our neo-constitutionalism agrees with the Confucian dichotomy between the ruling class and the ruled and seeks the immediate protection and achievement of liberty and human rights before the full development of constitutional democracy. It stresses benevolent government as the current constitutionalism stresses democracy. We view democracy as a distant ideal of mankind and urge current attention to human rights and the realization of benevolent government. In this aspect, there are many common points between what we call neo-constitutionalism and the classical Confucian government path.

The government path in the *Analects* was particularly concerned with moral standards of government. (*zheng*) Among such standards, benevolence was the most important. 'To exercise government by means of a ruler's virtue'[56] was the correct path of government. Ji Kangzi asked Confucius about the issue of government, saying, 'What do you think about killing the unprincipled for the good of the principled?' (*ru sha wu dao, yi jiu you dao, he ru*?) Confucius replied, 'Sir, in carrying on your government, why should you use killing at all? Let your evident desires be for what is good, and the people will be good. The relationship between superiors and inferiors is like that between the wind and the grass. The grass must bend when the wind blows across it.'[57] Government with benevolence and morality was the goal of the Confucian government path. The argument of the government path was raised against cruel and inhuman tyranny. Confucius said, 'If good men were to govern a country in succession for a hundred years, they would be able to transform the violently bad, and dispense with capital punishment. True indeed is this saying!'[58] It was a Confucian idea to oppose rulers who killed the innocent. Confucius said, 'Virtue is more to man than either water or fire. I have seen men die from treading on water and fire, but I have never seen a man die from treading the course of virtue.'[59]

Power is the main focus of the government path. However, the *Analects* focused on the restriction of the rulers' power by moral standard rather than by the legal system, as in the West. The *Analects* laid stress on self-control. Confucius said, 'To govern means to rectify. If you lead the people with correctness, who will dare not to be correct?'[60] 'When a prince's personal conduct is correct, his government is effective without the issuing of orders. If his personal conduct is not correct, he may issue orders, but they will not be followed.'[61]

'He was to attend carefully to the weights and measures, examine the body of the laws, restore the discarded officers, and the good government of the kingdom took its course.'[62]

Although the *Analects* talked about restricting rulers by compulsory norms, they were not so much legal norms as ethical ones. 'By extensively studying all learning, and keeping himself under the restraint of the rules of propriety, one may thus likewise not err from what is right.'[63] 'The Master, by orderly method, skillfully led men on. He enlarged my mind with learning, and taught me the restraints of propriety.'[64] If the restraints of propriety were combined effectively with the restraints of laws and both put in force at the same time, then the goal of restricting power would be achieved.

Modern party politics is quite different from politics in ancient times. When modern constitutionalism first appeared, party politics had not yet been fully developed. Nevertheless, no nation-state today is free of the influence of parties. Although the 'party' discussed in the *Analects* is different from the modern political party, the following reasoning is still of contemporary significance: (1) 'The faults of men are characteristic of the class to which they belong.'[65] (2) The more parties exist, the less benevolence there is (*dang er bu ren, ren er bu dang*). A party's ideology inevitably excludes benevolent ideas. This is the key reason why a party makes mistakes. (3) Parties should be eliminated and a man of noble character should never join a party.

The three points mentioned above showed that the *Analects* treated political parties basically as 'private parties' (fellow-villagers and neighbours — *si dang*). A party was inevitably for its own interest. The interest of any party or faction was just private interest, as opposed to public interest. The argument that a party somehow embodies the public interest cannot be seen in the *Analects*.

Our forefathers never imaged that the party politics of later ages would allow specific parties to manipulate the destiny of nation-states and peoples. In this aspect, Rousseau had thought about party problems more deeply than Confucius. Like Confucius, Rousseau was critical of political parties believing all parties reflected special private interest. Bearing this in mind, Rousseau advocated either eliminating parties absolutely or allowing the existence of numerous parties. In this way, it might be possible to prevent a party from replacing public opinion with its private interest. Multi-party competition has become a much more universal way to reflect public opinion than the one-party dictatorship. Confucian logic would lead to a similar conclusion and would certainly not support the notion of a one-party dictatorship.

Viewed from the perspective of constitutional theory, the idea in the *Analects* of recommending both the worthy and the well-known person should become the fundamental principle of our electoral system. Confucius said, 'Employ first the services of your various officers, pardon small faults, and raise to office men of virtue and talent.' (*xian you si, she xiao guo, ju xian cai*) But Zi Lu asked, 'How shall I know the men of virtue and talent, so that I may raise them to office?' Confucius continued, 'Raise to office those whom you know. As to those whom you do not know, will others neglect them?'[66]

Of course, the selection system talked about in the *Analects* mainly meant that the worthy person was only chosen by those persons in authority; it neglected the universality of suffrage. Under the current election system in China, the constituency is usually forced to vote for candidates with whom they are not familiar. 'The recommendation of the well-known' becomes the election of the unknown. As a result, this process cannot pursue the sensible course of 'recommending the worthy' and 'making the crooked act to be upright'. In order to carry out the principle of recommending the worthy, a regime should, as is generally done in modern democracies, allow campaigns for office so that the people can fully know the elected.

The government path discussed above may provide a theoretical basis for the development of constitutional government in China. A nation-state is inevitably made up by the ruling and ruled classes; we should not seek the so-called democracy in which everyone is the master but seek to have a benevolent government; governmental power must be restricted; leaders should restrict themselves at first; the superior man should attend carefully to weights and measures, examine the body of laws and restore discarded officers; the defect of a party is the lack of benevolence.

Conclusion

The Paths of Benevolence, Tolerance, Justice, and Government in the *Analects* constitute the basic contents and principles of the traditional system of benevolence theory, while the corresponding concepts of the ideologies of human rights, tolerance, resistance, and neo-constitutionalism make up the basic contents and principles of the new theory of benevolence we have advanced herein. What we call the new theory of benevolence is rooted in the traditional one and thus in Chinese soil. The close relationship between the *Analects'* four paths and the four principles of the new theory of benevolence provides a bridge between classical Chinese culture and modern human rights.

Notes

* All translations (with some revision) of the Confucian *Analects* is taken from James Legge (ed.) *The Chinese Classics, Vol. I: Confucian Analects, The Great Learning, The Doctrine of the Mean*, Hong Kong: University of Hong Kong Press, 1960.
1. Du Gangjian, 'The Ideology of Human Rights and Socialism,' (unpublished manuscript), (1992).
2. Du Gangjian, 'On the Ideology of Human Rights,' in *Lanzhou Journal of Studies*, No. 5, (1992).
3. Yanyuan Essay, No. 12, (*Fanchi wen ren, zi yue, 'ai ren'*).
4. Xue Er Essay, No. 1, (*Fan ai zhong, er qin ren*).
5. Yanyuan Essay, No. 12, (*Si hai zhi nei, jie xiong di ye*).
6. Xue Er Essay, No. 1, (*Xiao di ye zhe, qi wei ren zhi ben yu*).
7. Weizheng Essay, No. 2, (*Jin zhi xiao zhe, shi wei neng yang, zhi yu quan ma, jie neng you yang; bu jing, he yi bie hu?*).
8. Liren Essay, No. 4, (*Gou zhi yu ren yi, wu wu ye*).
9. Liren Essay, No. 4, (*Wei ren zhe neng hao ren, neng wu ren*).
10. Du Gangjian, 'On Elimination of Nihilism of Human Rights', in *Study of Law*, No. 1, (1992).
11. Yanyuan Essay, No. 12, (*Ai zhi yu qi sheng, wu zhi yu qi si. Ji yu qi sheng, you yu qi si, shi huo ye*).
12. Lirun Essay, No. 4, (*Fu zi zhi dao, zhong shu er yi yi*).
13. Weiling Gong Essay, No. 15, (*You yi yan er ke yi zhong shen xing zhi zhe hu? Qi shu hu! Ji suo bu yu, wu shi yu ren*).
14. Zizhang Essay, No. 15.
15. Yanghuo Essay, No. 17, (*Neng xing wu zhe yu tian xia wei ren yi, gong, kuan, xin, min, hei*).
16. Xue Er Essay, No. 1, (*Li zhi yong, he wei gui*).

17. Zi Lu Essay, No. 13, (*Jun zi he er bu tong, xiao ren tong er bu he*).
18. Guishi Essay, No. 16, (*Gai jun wu pin, he wu gua, an wu qing*).
19. Weiling Gong Essay, No. 15, (*Jun zi bu yi yan ju ren, bu yi ren fei yan*).
20. Xian Wen Essay, No. 14, (*You de zhe bi you yan, you yan zhe bu bi you de*).
21. Gong Zhichang Essay, No. 5, (*Shi wu yu ren, ting qi yan er xin qi xing; jin wu yu ren ye, ting qi yan er guan qi xing*).
22. Rao Yuan Essay, No. 20, (*Bu zhi yan, wu yi zhi ren ye*).
23. Wei Zi Essay, No. 18, (*Wu zhong, yi yi, yin ju fang yan, shen zhong qing, fei zhong quan. Wo ze yi yu shi, wu ke wu bu ke*).
24. Weizheng Essay, No. 2, (*Duo wen que yi, shen yan qi yu, ze gua you; duo jian que dai, shen xing qi yu, ze gua hui; yan gua you, xing gua hui, lu zai qi zhong yi*).
25. Yanghuo Essay, No. 17, (*Yu yu bu yan, ze xiao yu he shu yan? Zi he shu yan? Tian he yan zai? Si shi xing yan, bei wu sheng yan tian he yan zai*).
26. Xianwen Essay, No. 14, (*Bang you dao, wei yan wei xing; bang wu dao, wei xing yan sun*).
27. Shu Er Essay, No. 7, (*De zhi bu neng, xue yi bu jiang, wen yi bu neng tu, bu shan bu neng gai, shi wu you ye*).
28. Bashao Essay, No. 3, (*Cheng shi bu shuo, sui shi bu jian, ji wang bu jiu*).
29. Zi Lu Essay, No. 13, (*Xian you si, ju xian cai*).
30. Yong Ye Essay, No. 6, (*Bu qian nu, bu er guo*).
31. Du Gangjian, 'The Movement of Resistance in Legal Theory and the Idea of the Right to Resist,' in *Science of Law*, No. 3, (1992).
32. Suziki Kaifu, 'The Movement of April 19th and the Right to Resist,' paper presented in The International Conference on Constitutions and Democratic Politics, People's University of China, (1992).
33. Liren Essay, No. 4, (*Jun zi zhi yu tian xia ye, wu shi ye, wu mo ye, yi zhi yu bi*).
34. Xue Er Essay, No. 1, (*Xin jin yu yi, yan ke fu ye. Gong jin yu li, yuan chi ru ye*).
35. Gongye Chang Essay, No. 5, (*You jun zi zhi dao si yan: qi xing ji ye gong, qi shi shang ye jing, qi yang min ye hei, qi shi min ye yi*).
36. Yanyuan Essay, No. 12, (*Zhu zhong xin, tu yi, chong de ye. Ai zhi yu qi sheng, wu zhi yu qi si. Ji yu qi sheng, you yu qi si, shi huo ye*).
37. Yanyuan Essay, No. 12, (*Xian, shi hou de, fei chong de yu*).
38. Liren Essay, No. 4, (*Jun zi yu yu yi, xiao ren yu yu li*).
39. Zi Lu Essay, No. 13, (*Wu yu su, wu jian xiao li; yu su, ze bu da, jian xiao li ze da shi bu cheng*).

40. Weiling Gong Essay, No. 15, (*Jun zi yi yi wei zhi, li yi xing zhi, sun yi chu zhi, xin yi cheng zhi*).
41. Liren Essay, No. 4, (*Fu yu gui, shi ren zhi suo yu ye, bu yi dao de zhi, bu chu ye. Pin yu jian, shi ren zhi suo wu ye, bu yi qi dao de zhi, bu qu ye*).
42. Yanghuo Essay, No. 17, (*Jun zi yi yi wei sheng, jun zi you yong er wu yi wei luan, xiao ren you yong er wu yi wei dao*).
43. Xianwen Essay, No. 14, (*Jun zi dao zhe san: ren zhe bu you, zhi zhe bu huo, yong zhe bu ju*).
44. Xianwen Essay, No. 14, (*Ren zhe bi you yong, yong zhe bu bi you ren*).
45. Weizheng Essay, No. 2, (*Jian yi bu wei, wu yong ye*).
46. Yanyuan Essay, No. 12, (*Zhi zhi er hao yi*).
47. Weiling gong Essay, No. 15, (*Zhi zai shi yu! Bang you dao, ru shi; bang wu dao, ru shi*).
48. Wei Zi Essay, No. 18, (*Jun zi zhi shi ye, xing qi yi ye*).
49. Xianjin Essay, No. 11, (*Yi dao shi jun, bu ke ze zhi*).
50. Weiling Gong Essay, No. 15, (*Bang you dao, ze shi; bang wu dao, ze ke juan er huai zhi*).
51. Liren Essay, No. 4, (*Jun zi huai de, xiao ren huai du*).
52. Zi Lu Essay, No. 13, (*Ru bu shan er mo zhi wei ye, bu ji hu yi yan er sang bang hu*).
53. Zi Lu Essay, No. 13, (*Qi shen bu zheng, sui ling bu cong*).
54. Yaoyue Essay, No. 20.
55. Weiling Gong Essay, No. 15, (*Zhi shi ren ren, wu qiu sheng yi hai ren, you sha shen yi cheng ren*).
56. Weizheng Essay, No. 2, (*Wei zheng yi de*).
57. Yanyuan Essay, No. 12, (*Zi wei zheng, yan yong sha? Zi shan er min shan yi, jun zi zhi de feng, xiao ren zhi de cao, cao shang zhi feng*).
58. Zi Lu Essay, No. 13, (*Shan ren wei bang bai nian, yi ke yi sheng can qu sha yi. Cheng zai shi yan ye*).
59. Weiling Gong Essay, No. 15, (*Min zhi yu ren ye, shen yu shui huo. Shui huo, wu jian dao er si zhe yi, wei jian dao ren er si zhe ye*).
60. Yanyuan Essay, No. 12, (*Zheng zhe, zheng ye, zi shi yi zheng, shu gan bu zheng*).
61. Zi Lu Essay, No. 13, (*Qi shen zheng, bu ling er xing; qi shen bu zheng, sui ling bu cong*).
62. Yaoyue Essay, No. 20, (*Shen quan liang, shen fa du, xiu fei guan, si fang zhi zheng xing yan*).
63. Yanyuan Essay, No. 12, (*Bo xue yu wen, yue zhi yi li*).
64. Zihan Essay, No. 9, (*Da zi xun xun ran shan you ren, bo wo yi wen, yue wo yi li, yu ba bu neng*).
65. Liren Essay, No. 4, (*Ren zhi guo ye, ge yu qi dang*).
66. Zi Lu Essay, No. 13, (*Ju er suo zhi, er suo bu zhi, ren qi she zhu?*).

Part III
Contemporary Theories

Are Rights Culture-bound?

Margaret Ng

In this essay I wish to point out two common arguments which obscure the theory of human rights as it originated in classical liberalism. They are:

1)   the erroneous extension of the concept of rights to include 'welfare rights'; and
2)   the fallacy that 'human rights' are culture-bound, that 'Western' ideas of rights are unsuited to Asians.

While there has been a worldwide trend to extend the notion of human rights to include so-called welfare rights, as is evident in the International Covenant on Economic, Social and Cultural Rights, this trend is particularly promoted by socialist and developing countries and has become the primary theme in China's conception of rights. The argument that rights are culture-bound is promoted by some non-Western, especially Asian, governments and is likewise primary to China's conception of rights. These two related points are both prevalent themes in the Bangkok Declaration and are therefore of importance to the present discussion.

What Rights Are We Talking About?

When John Locke, John Stuart Mill, and other pre-twentieth century writers of liberalism wrote about rights, they were almost invariably talking about what would be called political and civil rights. These are 'negative' rights — i.e. the right not to be interfered with, and are thus synonymous with what Isaiah Berlin terms the 'negative' concept of liberty.[1] Put the other way round, as Quentin Skinner, who traced its origin to Hobbes, says, 'any theory of negative liberty must in effect be a theory of individual rights.'[2] In a famous passage, Mill says, 'The only freedom which deserves the name, is that of pursuing our own good in our own way, so long as we do not attempt to deprive others of theirs, or impede their efforts to obtain it.'[3] Freedom, of speech, of expression, of belief, of thought, of association, and so on, is freedom from intervention in these areas. It does not require anyone to do anything in the implementation of these rights except to refrain from interference.

This concept of rights is fundamentally focused on the rights of the individual against the government. Locke saw the right to liberty as the residual and inalienable right man is born with. He chose to put it in the vivid language of a social contract: 'Men being . . . by Nature, all free, equal and independent, no one can be put out of this Estate, and subjected to the Political Power of another, without his own Consent.'[4]

Not only is liberty a right which can only be surrendered with one's consent, but such consent is based on the enlightened self-interest of the individual and can impliedly be withdrawn. Moreover, this can never amount to a total and irrevocable surrender of natural liberty: 'For a Man, not having the Power of his own Life, cannot, by Compact, or his own Consent, enslave himself to anyone, nor put himself under the Absolute, Arbitrary Power of another, to take away his life, when he pleases.'[5]

To Mill, liberty is to be defended not only against the government but against all forms of the collective, that is all forms of encroachment of society upon the individual, whether by legislation or by force of opinion. Although he did not accept Locke's concept of natural rights and felt bound to speak in the language of utility, he nevertheless defended rights as the paramount utility: no society in which individual liberties are not respected can be free.

Thus, the concept of rights is quite clear in classical liberalism, and its strength lies in that clarity and its negative nature. All that anyone is required to do in respect of these rights is to leave others alone. These rights may not be all that is necessary to bring about the ideal society, but they are fundamental, axiomatic, and inviolate.

Basically the same concept of rights, the rights of the individual against the collective, is notably supported in contemporary thinking by Ronald Dworkin and Robert Nozick. In Dworkin's terms, 'A right against a government must be a right to do something even when the majority thinks it would be wrong to do it, and even when the majority would be worse off for having it done.'[6] Nozick opens his treatise with the statement, 'Individuals have rights, and there are things no person or group may do to them (without violating their rights).'⁷

Just as 'negative' rights arise from a negative concept of liberty, welfare rights arise, conceptually, from a positive concept of liberty: that to be free is not only to be unhindered, but also to be able to do certain things. There is no point in the freedom to hold my own belief or follow my own idea of the good life, if I am so poor and so deprived as to suffer from starvation, have no education, no opportunity to work, and lack other essentials to enable me to lead a decent life. Hence, to achieve freedom I must first enjoy the welfare fundamental to a decent life. This should be as much a right as the negative right to liberty.

In themselves entirely laudable, 'welfare rights' nevertheless obscure the concept of human rights in classical liberalism because these 'rights' are fundamentally different. For one thing, they are both 'positive' and aspirational. One should say, they are positive and therefore can only be aspirational.⁸

Welfare rights are positive in that they require other individuals to do something — my right to employment is someone's duty to employ (and presumably pay) me.⁹ My right to free medical service requires someone to provide the resources for it. This poses the obvious problem: who is going to provide the resources, and what if there are just not enough resources? And the reasonable answer must be, we do our best to get the resources, and in the meantime such 'rights' will be held in abeyance, and remain an aspiration. The only alternative to this is that some individuals be compelled to contribute.

The most profound distinction between these two concepts of rights lies in the concept of the individual behind each of them. To Locke, it is in man's nature that he is free, equal, and independent; that he 'has a Property in his own Person', and by extension, a property in the labour of his body and the work of his hands.¹⁰ To Mill, rights are 'grounded on the permanent interests of a man as a progressive being'.¹¹

Thus, one of the real conflicts between the concept of rights in classical liberalism and welfare rights is that it follows from the concept of welfare rights that the collective has a right to an individual's labour and how he pursues his life which is fundamentally repugnant to classical liberalism. The individual becomes, to a certain extent, owned by the collective. Still further, in justifying such a right to him, the advocates of welfare rights have to postulate a theory of the individual as distinct and separate from all his attributes.

The extension of human rights to include welfare rights has a profound effect on the whole theory of rights. It brings in the concept of priority. Rights are no longer immediate and compelling. They become a matter of agenda and collective planning. By expanding the concept of rights, we have lost our rights altogether.

What needs to be pointed out is that even if 'welfare rights' are to be accepted as a new species of 'rights', they must be recognized as secondary to political and civil rights. They are not on a par. They may be an addition to them, but not a substitute. There should be no question of violating a fundamental right in the name of advancing an aspiration, as the modern trend in the discussion of rights appears to advocate.

Another profound effect of this development is that it gives rise to the fallacy that rights are culture-bound and subject to the decision of the government of each nation. It is an easy step to take. If rights are a matter of aspiration and priority, then it would appear all too reasonable that each community should decide for itself what its priorities are, considering both its practical circumstances and common values.

In the midst of all this one forgets the most important point about rights, and that is, they belong to the individual. You may not violate the least of these rights, even to benefit a thousand. This, I take as the starting point of the present discussion.

Are Rights Culture-bound?

The trend in the twentieth century is to argue that human rights be based on 'universal standards'. The aim is to make it abundantly clear that these rights are more fundamental than the municipal laws of any state. They are not dependent upon municipal laws, nor can they be eliminated by them. They are in that sense 'universal'.

Yet at the same time as the advocacy of welfare rights there has developed the suggestion that rights are not universal, but merely a product of Western culture, and presumably applicable only to the West. To declare them 'universal', and to seek their implementation in Asia or Third World countries, is simply to impose the values of the West upon the non-Western world.

There is no doubt that this view is frequently advanced hypocritically by autocratic regimes for political purposes, for example, in the notorious Bangkok Declaration, but not invariably so. The interesting question is, why does such a view look so attractive to so many people who are by no means political hypocrites? In my view, the reason lies in that it has picked up two trends in modern discussions in social philosophy in general and rights in particular, and they are the influence of socialism on the concept of rights, resulting in the suggestion of welfare rights, and the idea of cultural pluralism.

Let me deal with cultural pluralism first, briefly. Pluralism is truly part of the liberal tradition. Indeed, it is the cornerstone of liberalism. It is the belief that each individual is entitled to define his own good. Cultural pluralism, one may be persuaded, is no more than an extension of individual pluralism. Different cultures have different systems of values. Only the cultural chauvinist would seek to impose the criteria of judgement of his own culture on that of another.

Thus it appears no more than a substitution of an axiom to say that the concept of human rights is a product of Western culture, and Westerners should not impose their standards on non-Western societies which may have different values.

However, this is a fallacy. Individuals living in a society and nations dealing with one another in the international community are by no means comparable, because the relationship between the individual and the State is not mirrored by the relationship between a particular state and whatever international organization there is. Cultures and societies are not 'super-individual' made up of units of individuals. Where rights are concerned, there are just the individual and the collective interest; if you take 'rights' as typically civic rights, rights are about the protection of the individual against the collective interest.

Some would say that the view I have just expressed is typical of Western individualism, but individualism is alien to Chinese culture, and so a theory of rights founded on such individualism will find no support in Chinese society. As Professor Gong Xiangrui of Beijing University described it in a recent presentation at the University of Hong Kong:

> In China, it is the state that comes first, the collective second, and the individual the last. If any conflict should occur, the collective benefit (such as that of the family, the school and the union) should be sacrificed for the state's interest: similarly, the individual's personal interest should give way to the interest of the collectives and the state. This proposition has been consistently maintained from the time of Sun Yatsen to that of Mao Zedong; it has its historical background too. Old China was a country oppressed by the great Powers — the imperialists. For example, Hong Kong island was ceded to the United Kingdom under the unequal Treaty of Nanking. Therefore, the first objective of the revolution was to attain independence and liberation of the nation. Although great changes have taken place since 1949, and the Chinese people are now standing up, independently and equally, among the nations, the above beliefs remain the same. A popular saying is that under socialism the interest of the state, of the collective, and of the individuals are in general harmony. If any conflict arises, the interests of the individual are subject to those of the collectives and the state. Putting the individual first is sometimes called individualism, and sometimes condemned as 'bourgeois-liberalization'.

But there is nothing 'Chinese' or even 'Asian' about socialism, inherently a Western invention. And the decades from Sun Yatsen to Mao Zedong are only a flash in China's long history.

Wang Gungwu goes much further both in terms of time and depth in describing the strangeness of the concept of the rights of the individual to Chinese social and political thought, from the time of Confucius down to contemporary, post-Cultural Revolutionary China, approaching the question linguistically and historically.[12] In his view, there was a kind of concept of rights in prototypical Confucianism — not expressed, but implied — to be found in the interwoven ideas of hierarchy and reciprocity. Since duties are prescribed for every level of the social hierarchy from common folk to ruler, and since the entitlement of the superior to the obedience of the inferior is reciprocal with the superior doing what is proper for his or her inferior, there is a kind of right there:

'... The subject's rights were expressed in terms of the rules of propriety due to him, and the ruler's rights in terms of the subject's loyalty which he could expect. . . . Propriety and loyalty were not simply duties; they were also, implicitly, rights in a given reciprocal relationship.'[13]

Nevertheless, in his view, whatever 'rights' there were in that system, they never developed into anything like the Western idea of the rights of the individual acting as a check on the government's absolute power. The main reason was the consolidation of absolute power in China; and in the nineteenth century, even when rights and democracy began to attract intellectuals, they could only see rights in terms of *zhu quan* (sovereignty) or *min quan* (rights/power of the people). Rights were seen as the kind of power China needed for regeneration, as instrumental, and as belonging to the collective, for example, the class of common people.

However, though Wang does not see the 'Western' concept of rights developing in China in the immediate future, he does not put forward any theory that because it was historically, or even linguistically absent, the concept of rights is somehow inappropriate for China or the Chinese.

For one has to distinguish between the origins of rights theories, the validity of rights theories, and the implementation of rights. While it may be said that rights theories, at least those most often discussed, and certainly those represented as classical liberalism in the present discussion, have their origins in the writings of the West, it does not follow that they therefore express Western values, only suitable for and applicable to the West. Writers of classical liberalism, in so far as they were original thinkers, were not reporting values prevalent in their society (they were if anything attacking contrary values), but rather proposing principles which they believed should be recognized as having universal validity. Whether they should be accepted or rejected must depend on whether they are valid or invalid, not whether they originate from the West or the East.

Neither is the question of implementation — whether rights should be enforced in each state and how — relevant. It cannot affect the validity of rights theories, although implementation would no doubt be strongly urged if the rights theories are accepted to be valid.

Rights and the Chinese Tradition

Bearing the above in mind, one may say that in one sense the concept of rights is alien to the Chinese tradition. It goes without saying that there is not one single 'Chinese tradition' but several, as is amply demonstrated by Wang Gungwu's paper referred to above. Even when one refers to the mainstream tradition of Confucianism, it goes without saying that it is not one immutable body of thinking but an evolving one, split into many schools, developed through time and in response to various stimuli. Such stimuli include Buddhism and Western philosophy which, though frequently conflicting, were frequently subjected to attempts at reconciliation and synthesis. Thus to generalize is to court the facile and superficial, unless one is extremely alert to its limits.

One can generalize to some extent about Confucianism at its broadest and most fundamental, which includes features which are not only common to the different schools but distinct in prototype, i.e. Confucianism as it is manifest in its primary source, the Confucian *Analects*. Such generalization may be stated as follows: Confucian morality is a chivalrous morality, a morality based on the class distinction between the uneducated common folk, the 'little man', and the aristocracy, the educated elite, the 'princely man'. The small man has needs; the princely man has obligations. The rules of moral conduct, central to which lies one's duty to the community, are founded on the concept of *noblesse oblige*, i.e., the responsibility that comes with privilege. The well-being of the state rests upon princely men who fill its ruling positions observing that very high standard of moral conduct. Conversely, the princely man's voluntary observance of such a moral code, for no other reason than that he is noble, is thought to be sufficient guarantee for the well-being of society, meaning the welfare of the little men, the common folk.

In such a scheme there is no need — and therefore no room — for rights. The princely man has not rights but privileges which he does not need to assert. The little man is amply looked after without his ever raising his voice in demand, since his welfare is the duty of his social superiors who rule the state. It is an effrontery to speak to the princely man of the rights of the people, because it implies that rights are necessary, and rights are necessary only if the princely man cannot be trusted to perform his obligations.

From this point of view, rights are certainly alien to Chinese tradition. Yet this is a far cry from proving any rights theory must be an imposition of Western culture and values upon Chinese culture, and therefore must be wrong because of being chauvinistic.

The reason is simply this. The basis of such a moral code is itself chauvinistic and therefore unacceptable. Moreover, the evolution from a chivalrous morality to an egalitarian one in the West is also relatively new. Isaiah Berlin remarked that individual liberty as a political ideal was comparatively modern, East or West, and that the domination of this ideal has been the exception rather than the rule, even in the recent history of the West.[14] There is nothing inherently alien about a similar evolution in the Chinese tradition which is, or should be, after all, a living thing.

Indeed, Confucius himself was in an important sense a 'liberal' in that he changed the very core idea of who is the 'princely man'. The princely man, before Confucius, was simply a son born of a prince. It was an accident of birth, and privileges sprang solely from birth. Confucius turned the princely man from someone superior by birth into someone superior by morality, much in the same way that philosophers of the West, many centuries later, were to do the same, by making 'virtue' not a matter of power but of moral excellence.

One may acknowledge that the concept of rights is generally 'alien' to the Chinese tradition in its *past and present state*. But this does not make out the case that rights are alien to Chinese society *by nature*. Nor does it establish that it is therefore legitimate to exclude Chinese society from the application of human rights.

Indeed, the fact that the concept of rights has hitherto been 'alien' to, or at any rate weak in, the Chinese tradition makes its introduction into Chinese society all the more pressing — just as its revival in the West became pressing in the face of utilitarian-based policies aimed at elevating the collective good at the expense of individual rights in the late nineteenth and early twentieth centuries.[15] When the rights of the individuals risk being lost sight of in wholesale social planning, there is the need to protect them by re-emphasizing their existence and importance. Likewise, Confucian *noblesse oblige* is seen as being either inadequate protection for the people, or simply unacceptable protection from the view of those it is aimed at protecting. This is simply because it is condescending and affords an unreliable sanction. Therefore serious efforts must be made to bring rights in as the next development in the Chinese tradition.

Unfortunately, though not surprisingly, this is not the direction present Chinese leaders have chosen to take. Indeed, everything is being done to resist the demand from within, by the Chinese people, for recognition of civil and political rights in China. Instead, under such pressure, Chinese leaders have recently chosen to respond by joining with a number of governments in Asia to make the Bangkok Declaration. The gist of this Declaration is to stress economic development as a right, and to assert that human rights, as far as Asian states have the right to decide for themselves, must come only after a certain level of economic development has been reached. To quote, the participating governments made the following Declaration:

> *Reiterating* the interdependence and indivisibility of eco-
> nomic, social, cultural, civil, and political rights, and the
> inherent interrelationship between development, demo-
> cracy, universal enjoyment of all human rights, and social
> justice which must be addressed in an integrated and bal-
> anced manner.
> *Recalling* that the Declaration on the Right to Development
> has recognized the right to development as a universal and
> inalienable right and an integral part of fundamental human
> rights.
> *Emphasizing* that endeavours to move towards the creation
> of uniform international human rights norms must go hand
> in hand with endeavours to work towards a just and fair
> world economic order.
> *Convinced* that economic and social progress facilitates the
> growing trend towards democracy and the promotion and
> protection of human rights.[16]

In other words, what it says is that civil rights can only be considered after welfare rights have been taken care of. Rights are in any event an imposition of Western values on Asian states, which have greater need for economic development than for the protection of individual rights, and the proper role of the West is not to criticize Asian states for falling short of such a Western ideal, but rather to provide economic aid towards that development.

The political purpose behind such a stance is too obvious to require comment. If it is worthy of serious criticism at all, it is because of the link, as far as China is concerned, between this stance and the thinking of late nineteenth-century Chinese intellectuals discussed by Wang Gungwu and referred to above, that the rights of the people are important essentially because recognizing such rights helps to strengthen China as a nation. The vulnerability of that earlier rights theory is, of course, that it makes rights conditional upon their pragmatic value. This means they are easily sacrificed should their recognition threaten to bring trouble, at least according to the government.

It is significant that the Bangkok Declaration chooses to see rights not as belonging to individuals, but to the collective — the State. From the viewpoint of classical liberalism, this is plainly wrong and makes nonsense of the whole *raison d'être* of the theory of rights. In utilitarian terms, this says that we can justify allowing some members of society to suffer to achieve greater pleasure for others by saying a person often chooses to suffer a little now for the sake of later and greater pleasure. John Rawls points out the fallacy in this argument as being its adoption 'for society as a whole the principle of rational choice for one man'.[17] Nozick put it even more bluntly, 'There is no social entity with a good that undergoes some sacrifice for its own good. There are only individual people.'[18] Using one of these people for the benefit of others is to use him to benefit others, no more.

The predominantly Chinese society in Hong Kong has responded quite favourably to the increased protection of human rights under the new Hong Kong Bill of Rights Ordinance. This ordinance incorporates the language of the International Covenant on Civil and Political Rights. This support for the International Covenant refutes the argument that rights are 'alien' to Asians.

The heart of the popular debate is rather the classical question — what are the limits of the rights enshrined, and how does one balance the freedom of the individual against the good of the community? In short, where does your freedom end and my rights begin? The deepest concern so far expressed is the effect on law and order. For example, will the power of the police be so curtailed as to make it difficult for them to enforce the law? Will it mean guilty people will be let off unpunished? Hong Kong people are conviction-minded, favour a strong police force, have little real use for the presumption of innocence, and think rather less of the rights of foreigners than the rights of locals — just as people in England do. There is nothing particularly Chinese or Asian about any of these prejudices.

On the other hand, you would find among Hong Kong people a strong support for non-interference in other aspects. For example, for the freedom of speech and freedom of the press. Businessmen might think the press has gone too far on most days, and individual newspaper proprietors may well expect to practise a degree of self-censorship to stay out of trouble, but the wider public despises such positions. A reputation that a publication is not independent or practises self-censorship guarantees its circulation will go down.

Nothing in the reaction of the Hong Kong Chinese to human rights lends support to the view that this 'Western' concept is alien to them, that their 'rich culture' prompts them to support postponing the protection of rights until Hong Kong is richer or more socially stable. Even the less privileged in Hong Kong, the blue-collar worker, whose real wage increase is not catching up with inflation, and who is therefore keen on promoting some degree of 'welfare rights', does not sanction the suppression of civil liberties until such times as welfare levels have reached a certain goal.

Conclusion

Once it is accepted that political and civil rights are the only rights proper, as distinct from welfare rights which are aspirations, the fallacy of rights being culture-bound cannot be maintained. The negative nature of rights, and their universal validity, removes the excuse against their immediate and complete implementation. The true question is not whether each state may justifiably postpone the implementation of rights until certain economic conditions have been achieved. It is, rather, whether the State may legitimately violate the rights of the individual in order to attain such collective goals as economic development, or simply to safeguard the continued power of a particular government. There can be no doubt what the answer is.

Notes

1. Isaiah Berlin, 'Two Concepts of Liberty', 1969, reprinted in Michael J. Sandel (ed.), *Liberalism and Its Critics*, Oxford: Basil Blackwell Publisher Ltd., 1984, p. 15.
2. Quentin Skinner, 'The Idea of Negative Liberty', in Richard Rorty, Jerome B. Schneewind and Quentin Skinner (eds.) *Philosophy in History: Essays on the Historiography of Philosophy*, Cambridge: Cambridge University Press, 1984, Reprinted 1985, p. 203.
3. John Stuart Mill, 'On Liberty,' in Mary Warnack (ed.) John Stuart Mill, *Utilitarianism, On Liberty, Essay on Bentham*, London: Fontana Press, 1962, 17th Impression, 1985, p. 138.
4. John Locke, *The Second Treatise on Government*, Cambridge: Cambridge University Press, Reprinted 1993 Chapter VIII, para. 95.
5. *Ibid*, Chapter IV, para. 23.
6. Ronald Dworkin, *Taking Rights Seriously*, Cambridge: Harvard University Press, 1977, 4th Impression, 1984, p. 194.
7. Robert Nozick, *Anarchy, State, Utopia*, New York: Basic Books, 1974, 1984 Edition, Preface, p. ix.
8. The classical debate on political versus welfare rights between David D. Raphael and Maurice Cranston, in David D. Raphael (ed.), *Political Theory and the Rights of Man*, London: Macmillan Press, 1967.
9. For a discussion on how rights are related to duties, see the Introduction in Jeremy Waldron (ed.), *Theories of Rights*, Oxford: Oxford University Press, 1984.
10. Locke, *The Second Treatise on Government*, Chapter V, para. 27.
11. Mill, *On Liberty*, p. 136.
12. Wang Gungwu, *Power, Rights, and Duties in Chinese History*, Canberra: Australian National University, 1979, reprinted in Wang Gungwu, *The Chineseness of China*, Hong Kong: Oxford University Press, 1991.
13. *Ibid*, p. 171.
14. Berlin, 'Two Concepts of Liberty,' p. 21.
15. See Friedrich Hayak, chapter on 'Principles and Expediency', in Vol. 1, *Law, Legislation and Liberty*, London: Routledge & Kegan Paul, 1973, p. 55.
16. The Bangkok Declaration, *see* Appendix.
17. John Rawls, *A Theory of Justice*, Oxford: Clarendon Press, 1972, 1985 Edition, p. 27.
18. Nozick, *Anarchy, State Utopia*, p. 32.

Human Rights and
Non-Western Values

Eliza Lee

Philosophical discussions about human rights often evolve
around two contending camps, the universalists and the cultural relativists.[1] Universalists wish to ground the justification
of human rights on transcendental principles, such that
human rights are possessed by individuals independent of
time, place, and culture. Cultural relativists often view the
universalist claim as ideological. They see human rights (or
the conception of human rights which currently dominates
the international discourse) as cultural practices specific to
the 'West'. Any claim to universality is merely the imposition of Western moral standards onto other cultures, ethno-
centric if not often motivated by political interests.

I contend that the epistemological and theoretical foundations of both the universalist and the relativist positions
are inadequate. This essay draws upon theories of practice
and discourse to argue that the universalist aspiration for an
international normative order and the culturalist claim that
social and political orders are fundamentally cultural may
not be antithetical. Both claims suffer some limitations or
closure in that they take a static view of social and political
order, rather than considering how they are evolving.
International human rights practice is a process of discursive
formation. As Rolando Gaete states, in this post-modernist
sense:

> Human rights do not exist as heavenly and pure principles
> but as a specific discourse with ambivalent rules of forma-
> tion. It is this discourse that must be subjected to interro-
> gation. How are its meanings generated, who controls them,
> what statements are or can be censored or excluded? Are
> human rights reflexive, that is, do they control the state-
> ments interpreting them? What are the limits of the domain
> where statements on human rights are formed?[2]

This essay will concentrate on changing political norms
and relate this to the processes of assimilating human rights
values. First, it discusses the hermeneutic process of change

in political language and meaning as an integral part of a changing political order. Second, it contends that the assimilation of human rights practices in any cultural community requires the acceptance of the related core values. Instead of grounding human rights on some metaphysical claims or denying that they are associated with any particular political philosophy, one should recognize the historical and intellectual heritage of human rights in Western liberal democratic ideas. However, advancing human rights in non-Western communities, rather than resulting in Western cultural hegemony, may be seen as a process of rejuvenating the values of such non-Western communities through integration with the liberal values of autonomy and pluralism. Third, it discusses how the liberalism-communitarianism debate of the 1980s and 1990s has sparked off discussions on a number of issues: the conceptions of selfhood, autonomy, and individuality; the relationship between the individual and the community; and the role of the State. These discussions have important implications for human rights practices in non-Western communities (and particularly in Asia).

Politics as Practice — the Foundations of Political Order

The position of this article is that social and political orders are always in a process of change. As such, local communities should not be seen as closed, isolated, and homogeneous but as open to transformation. On the other hand, a community of shared norms may not be taken as pre-culturally or pre-politically given but as a historically evolving process. The role of language and communications — essentially the 'universal medium' of social and political life — is an important aspect of this process. Changes in political language and meaning through communication and dialogue are thus integral to the process of changing political order.

According to interpretative social science, all social life has to be understood as systems of cultural relationships. Social life proceeds as symbolic interaction governed by binding consensual norms which define reciprocal expectations about behaviour. The validity of social norms is grounded in the intersubjective understanding of intentions and secured by the general recognition of obligations among members of a community.[3]

Politics as a form of practice takes place in the same sociocultural logic. In Jurgen Habermas's terms, it belongs to the realm of symbolic interaction or communicative action. As a practical relationship it presupposes prior interactions, backgrounds of shared understandings and recognized norms and institutions, joining interacting parties. In this sense, the nature of political order is normative; its basis is linguistic; and its process of formation is communicative.

As such, human beings are not just objects of political order. They are ultimately the subjects, if not the authors, of that order. The normative nature of political order means that it is ultimately based on norms and meanings that are intersubjectively understood and collectively accepted. In this sense, all political order has a transformative potential. All transformation takes place within traditions and discourse communities. Changes in political norms and meanings are a matter of changes in tradition if not changes in subjectivity. These take place as processes of discourse, either between rival traditions or within a tradition.

The Limitations of 'Universalism' and 'Relativism'

The Universalist Position

The universalist position is predicated upon a concept of basic human nature in which rights are independent of time, place, culture, ideology, or value systems. This conceptualization, which can be called 'essentialist', varies for different theories, but it appeals in all its forms at the philosophical level to some common conditions of human existence. These essentialist notions may include the idea of human beings as moral beings, the concept of dignity, or an 'appeal' to common needs. It is in these senses that human rights are often argued as being both 'pre-cultural' and 'pre-political'.

The universalist position is often regarded as having an important connection with the Western historical foundation of human rights. To highlight some of its important sources, it is traceable back to the Western 'natural law' tradition of the Graeco-Roman culture. The modern tradition is distinguished by its individualist foundation. The natural rights theory of John Locke is an individualistic theory of rights, which claims that individuals possess by nature the rights to life, liberty, and property. Emmanuel Kant's 'categorical imperative' is based on the metaphysical notion of the individual as an autonomous being who makes his own choices. The Enlightenment takes as its theme the liberation of humankind from all forms of authority and tradition through the common faculty of reason.

It is often argued that these heritages form the background of the Universal Declaration of Human Rights and the human rights ideal of the twentieth century. There is still much controversy as to how rights can be 'universal' and 'inalienable'.[4] Nonetheless, in general, the justification of the universality of human rights, according to the universalists, lies in the ability to ground the value and knowledge of the human rights claim on bases that are not contingent upon culture, tradition, or one's place in history. Non-Western states often criticize (on the grounds of these ideological beliefs) the idea of universal human rights as an imposition of Western values and biases.

The Relativist Position

The relativist position is that we can only understand and evaluate social actions by reference to the rules and norms that are internal to that culture. Standards of evaluation are internal to traditions. There cannot be a standard of judgement independent of a given form of life and no single tradition is in a position to arbitrarily impose its own standards onto another tradition. In the context of cultural pluralism, this would amount to ethnocentrism. Stated in the most positive terms possible, cultural relativism is cultural egalitarianism in a multi-cultural world. Few relativists would argue that there are no common norms of any kind in the international community today. Nonetheless, human rights are those kinds of normative standards that are largely internal to each cultural tradition.[5]

Cross-cultural Universalism

Others, instead of grounding human rights on metaphysical claims about human nature, may adopt cross-cultural empirical studies to identify values and norms that are shared by all cultures. The central question, they contend, is whether other cultures have a concept of human rights. Even if non-Western societies do not express moral concerns in a framework of human rights, they may nonetheless address them in their own conceptual frameworks. Often scholars appeal to some common general conditions that they have identified across cultural or political systems, i.e. there are always normative principles that place limits on what individuals may do to one another and what a government may do to its citizens. The key then is to establish structural equivalents or comparable notions for human rights in other societies and cultural systems.[6]

The methodological problem of the cross-cultural universalist position is one of identifying common reference points from which to establish equivalents across cultures. This is actually the problem of all cross-cultural or comparative studies. It is not the aim of this paper to discuss this issue in depth. However, the general problem of the comparative approach is that it often assumes that the identification of reference points is itself unproblematic. The truth is that the reference points are often themselves culturally biased. This leads us back to the challenge of cultural relativism that there are no neutral reference points applicable across cultures from which to understand social and political phenomena.

The general limitation of the universalist and relativist mode of thinking is the way they treat political order as static and unchanging. Universalists assume that political values must be pre-cultural, pre-political givens if they are to have universal validity, thus overlooking the fact that any political community is historically and culturally constituted. Cultural relativists, ironically, while arguing against universalism end up adopting a similar logic — taking the existing order as valid and as static and unchanging. Cross-cultural universalism still fails to provide a framework for understanding cultural communities as discourse communities.

Traditions as Continuously Evolving Discourse Communities

It is a grave misunderstanding to assume that emphasis on the essential factor of tradition which enters into all understanding implies an uncritical acceptance of tradition and sociopolitical conservatism. . . . In truth the confrontation of our historic tradition is always a critical challenge of this tradition. . . . Every experience is such a confrontation.[7]

We are never locked within a single grammar. Rather, the first grammar that we learn to master already puts us in a position to step out of it and to interpret what is foreign, to make comprehensible what is incomprehensible, to assimilate in our own words what at first escapes them.[8]

One fallacy of the doctrine of cultural relativism is its oversimplification of the unity of traditions, assuming that they each have closed, concrete boundaries and are internally free of conflicts. In fact, at any time, a tradition may be faced with critics and rivals, both externally and internally. A tradition is thus not a static, harmonious whole, but a continuously evolving discourse community. It may change over the course of time as 1) the tradition comes into self-understanding and self-knowledge, from unreflected to reflective understanding of its practices; 2) it engages in internal questioning of the coherence of its doctrines, or of the inherited interpretation of authoritative texts or utterances, or even as a result of disputes over who the authoritative interpreter(s) should be; 3) it encounters other communities; or 4) changes in material conditions cause new issues to emerge.[9]

Also, the existence of rival traditions or rivalry within a tradition does not preclude the possibility of rational communication. Richard Bernstein has advanced the argument against confusing the problem of rival traditions with relativism. Essentially, the 'incommensurability' of paradigms or traditions does not entail relativism. The incommensurability thesis does refute objectivism in that it holds that there is no neutral framework or language that can be used to evaluate rival paradigms and that can be used in a point-by-point comparison between them. Nevertheless, rational debate and argumentation between proponents of rival paradigms and traditions is not impossible. In fact, that two rival traditions can meaningfully disagree with each other presupposes some overlapping of concepts, standards, and problems.[10]

More importantly, the presence of incommensurable paradigms and rival traditions is precisely the possible condition for the transformation of traditions. The most important

potential gain from understanding other cultures and societies is the consequences it has for our own self-understanding.
'It is the beginning of wisdom to realize that what we take
to be intuitive, natural, obvious, or universal may not be so
at all but is only one historical social possibility among several alternatives.' We attain self-knowledge 'whenever we realize that something that we have thought was obvious, universal,
and intuitive may not have this epistemological character at
all.' As Peter Winch states:

> What we may learn by studying other cultures are not
> merely possibilities of different ways of doing things. . . .
> More importantly we may learn different possibilities of
> making sense of human life, different ideas about the pos-
> sible importance that the carrying out of certain activities
> may take on for a man, trying to contemplate the sense of
> his life as a whole.[11]

Thus, there is no human understanding that is free from historical or cultural contexts, that is, all understandings take
place within traditions. On the other hand, confrontation of
rival traditions creates the opportunity for a deeper, more
critical understanding of our own forms of life and even
uncovers our prejudices. In other words, self-knowledge and
self-understanding are attained through the discursive space
that is opened up for critical reflection. As Bernstein puts it,
'the "truth" of the incommensurability thesis is not closure
but *openness*.'

At this point, there is a need to explore more deeply into
the dialogical process between rival traditions. Here I draw
upon the knowledge of hermeneutics and the post-modern
notion of the interaction between the reader and the text.
One fundamental conclusion that can be drawn is that the
attainment of understanding between two different traditions
operates according to a dialogical/communicative logic, which
is also a logic of interpretive understanding.

According to Gadamar's hermeneutics, the appreciation of
a work of art is not a passive process of the work standing
apart from a spectator. Rather, there is a dynamic interaction between the work and the spectator. The same logic
applies to any case of interaction between a 'text' and its
'reader'. The meaning of a text is realized only when it is
understood. Understanding, in other words, is intrinsic to
the meaning of the text. Understanding is a part of the process

of the coming into being of meaning. In this sense, the process of understanding is never finished. Self-knowledge is achieved in the dialectical interplay with the 'other,' the process Gadamar refers to as the 'fusion of horizons'.[12] Through the fusion of horizons, our own horizon is enlarged and enriched.

The possibility of such fusion is due to the essential openness of language. A tradition is always subject to reinterpretation. In fact, our understanding of our own history, tradition, and culture confronts us as 'texts' whose meanings are not completed without our 'reading' them as historical beings. Each generation brings new understanding to their own tradition and culture through the development, if not imaginative innovation, of new concepts, language, and experiences. If, as previously argued, the foundation of political order is in shared norms and meanings, the emergence of a new political order is then a historically situated meaning-production process.

The Core Values of Contemporary Human Rights Practices

As discussed, there are multiple sources of contemporary human rights practices. Contemporary international human rights standards, as various international documents provide, include substantial input from non-Western nations and other ideological heritages. For instance, Marxist regimes have a strong commitment to social and economic equality while de-emphasizing private property rights, while many Third World countries place great emphasis on cultural and political self-determination. Nonetheless, it cannot be denied that Western liberalism has been significant in constituting the content of the international human rights regime. This is especially true concerning the aspects of civil and political rights.

More importantly, the international human rights regime, while compatible with the values and practices of many cultural communities, is not neutral in the sense of not presupposing any particular conception of the good. The four distinct categories of rights in the Universal Declaration — civil rights, political rights, social and economic rights, and cultural rights — read as a whole, provide an institutional order that upholds particular political values. Among them are values that are pertinent to Western liberal democratic regimes but not necessarily to other cultural communities — for instance, values such as freedom, pluralism, equality, and justice. In this sense, the problem of adopting human rights practices in many of these non-Western regimes requires the critical confrontation, if not integration, of liberal values with their own cultural practices. In many cases, the result might even be the inevitable exclusion of certain political and cultural practices. However, it does not follow that non-Western societies must give up all their cultural heritage if they adopt the idea of human rights. Nor is it the case that the adoption necessarily means the hegemonic imposition and brutal transplantation of alien practices to an ethnic community. Rather, human rights practices may be integrated with a variety of cultural practices, and the process of change may be through the members of those communities reflecting on their own traditions and historical experiences.

Reconsidering the Philosophical Foundation of Liberalism: the Liberalism-Communitarianism Debate

Many non-Western nations have argued that adopting human rights values is tantamount to accepting Western individualism, which would destroy the social and political order of their communities. Prominent examples include some Islamic beliefs and practices which are argued to be in conflict with such human rights norms as gender equality, religious freedom, and even freedom from torture. In many other communities, the ideas of equality between the sexes may be in tension with cultural practices such as property inheritance along the male line, arranged marriage, female circumcision, etc. Culturalists argue that these practices are integral and constitutive of cultural systems, and that they cannot be changed without destroying the integrity of the communal order. For some cultural heritages, the whole community order may be based on the idea of hierarchy and communalism rather than equality or individual freedom.

One fundamental issue in this controversy is, then, the

conflict of human rights standards, especially their liberal values, with community values. In fact, the problem of theoretical conflicts between liberalism and a sense of community has recently also been of concern to Western scholars. The academic debates of the 1980s between liberalism and communitarianism is paradigmatic of this debate.

The critique of liberalism as advanced by communitarians such as Michael Sandel, Alasdair MacIntyre, Charles Taylor, Michael Walzer, and others, centres around the liberal conception of the self, its relationship with the community, and also the role of the State.[13] Their attack was mostly on rights-based liberalism advanced mainly by such liberal philosophers as John Rawls and Robert Nozick.[14] The communitarian critique of liberalism points out that the ideal liberal self, as a subject of choice, is an individual who is antecedently individuated, 'disengaged,' or 'unencumbered'. Individual values, goals, and identity are the results of willful and voluntary choice and subjective expressions of preference. Preferences are autonomously chosen, so that individual identity is not constituted by communities or any value or conception of the good.

In response to such claims, communitarians advance a communally oriented conception of the person. Charles Taylor argues that selfhood is ineluctably a social product. People can only form their identities and their sense of individuality from the social matrix within which they happen to reside. Human beings are self-interpreting animals in linguistic communities. They make sense of themselves as persons and moral agents through concepts and standards bequeathed to them by practices and traditions; they come to know and define who they are through conversations with the social others; they are culture-producing and culture-inhabiting creatures. Alasdair MacIntyre advances the concept of *telos* that constitutes the good of a whole human life. Human beings make sense of their lives through the attainment of narrative unity. This narrative is not simply individual, but is and must be seen as communal. Social relationships are defined and formed within the traditions of social groups. The history of one's life cannot be told apart from one's membership in a social group or community, and also the relationships one establishes by virtue of that membership.

The problem of liberalism is thus its lack of a theory of

the community. If we adopt the abstract individualism of liberalism, the liberal selves are bound to be atomized, moral solipsists, holding communities to be only of instrumental value for the pursuit of personal interests. Of political significance, this definition of the self as a subject of free choice obscures how our sense of well-being, our values, our conceptions of the good life, our senses of who we are and what we might become, and even our life chances are defined by social relationships.

Furthermore, the liberal state claims that it should stay neutral among competing conceptions of the good. This means that it does not get involved in substantive debate as to the value of particular ways of life, for what is valued is the primacy of individuals' freedom to make their own choices. The dependence of individual autonomy on the particular social matrix in which one resides means however that public policies, especially on aspects of distributive justice, always involve judgement of the good.

Communitarian critics, while exposing the theoretical shortcomings of liberalism, have not failed to recognize the values of freedom, equality, justice, etc., that are advanced by the doctrine. They have no intention of endorsing the values of tradition and community to such an extent as to render an individual's identity and autonomy totally defined by the collectivity, the potential oppressiveness of which is fully recognized.

The emerging research program in this debate is the reconciliation of individual autonomy with community, or the integration of liberalism and communitarianism. Communitarians have no intention of endorsing the way traditional communities have ascribed individuals their social role based on hierarchy, if not outright domination and subordination. Nor do they think that individuals should be coerced into staying in one social group and not be allowed to question, if not to challenge, the inherent traditions of their communities.[15]

Liberal theorists, on the other hand, have worked to bring the community back into their theories. John Rawls in his later works has abandoned the idea that his principles of justice are the universal outcome of the free choices that rational individuals could be expected to make when they come together and are put behind the 'veil of ignorance'.[16] Instead, he recognizes that the liberal self and the principles of justice as fairness are constituted in the context of a liberal democratic regime. Its citizens are supposed to have a shared sense of understanding of society as a fair scheme of co-operation between free and equal citizens. With this shared aim, the liberal state is not that kind of political community united under one comprehensive (religious, philosophical, or moral) doctrine of the good, but is one that allows for the coexistence of multiple communities and conceptions of the good. Thus the historical character of liberalism is recognized. Western liberalism is itself a form of political culture. The liberal self is a modern experience, constituted by and only made possible within a liberal community. Individual rights are not universal in the sense of existing prior to any political community. Instead, rights are forms of social practice. Joseph Raz in *The Morality of Freedom* explicitly argues that liberalism is a form of political community that constitutes a particular type of social individual, and with a particular conception of the good. The liberal State is not a neutral State. Its core value, and thus its role, is to enhance individual autonomy and pluralism.

However, autonomy and pluralism are now understood as socially constituted. Autonomy is not the natural state that individuals are in when left to exercise free choice. The ideal of individual autonomy is actually a strong theory of the good — that the good life is one in which individuals are the authors of their own lives. Autonomy is socially defined in that the goals, preferences, and values of individuals, in sum the meanings of individual activities, are derived from the shared social matrix. Meaningful autonomy requires the existence of various social goods which the State has the duty to provide and which the citizens have duties to provide one another.

This social conception of individual autonomy also stipulates that the liberal State must uphold the value of pluralism by allowing for, if not actually providing, the resources for the coexistence of multiple social forms, if true individual autonomy is to be realized. In the process, the liberal state cannot stay neutral among competing conceptions of the good. It cannot support all life forms equally but must decide (presumably through democratic participatory processes) on the distribution of resources and, in so doing, make judgements on what kinds of social goods to provide.[17]

Such reconstruction of the philosophical foundation of liberalism certainly raises complicated issues, from questions of public policies to the nature of freedom and equality itself, which cannot be discussed adequately in this essay. An important idea emerging from the debate, however, is that such classic liberal values as autonomy and pluralism are not at odds with community values. In fact, no social order is sustained merely by the idea of individual rights. The integration of liberal values and other community values is thus possible if not necessary. As Flathman states:

> We are not presented with a simple choice between rights-oriented individualism and community. We are presented, rather, with a complex admixture of practices, arrangements, institutions, and values and with choices as to the ways in which that mixture should be preserved and/or altered in particular respects. From this perspective there are respects in which the values of the practice of rights and those of community, however irreconcilable they may be in abstract formulation, can be not merely compatible but complementary and mutually supportive.[18]

Flathman points out that the rights-community dichotomy has been exaggerated and misrepresented. Indeed, even in Western societies, the political tradition is not merely liberal, but a mixture of many traditions that are unique to the history of different societies. (American political tradition for instance is a mixture of liberalism, republicanism, populism, Protestantism, etc.) Liberal rights have never been the sole constituents of social and political order. Other values such as friendship, love, generosity, gratitude, etc., have always been present. Nor is it true that social institutions are based solely on liberal values. The institution of monogamous marriage is an examples to prove the case.

Towards the Integration of Human Rights Practices with Non-Western Practices

So what are the implications of the liberalism-communitarianism debate on the problem of adopting human rights practices in non-Western societies? It seems that adopting the liberal values inherent in human rights practices may not be altogether in conflict with community values. However, it is also true that such values are bound to be in conflict with a lot of traditional practices. The liberal values of freedom, equality, autonomy, and pluralism are bound not to be compatible with traditional practices such as hierarchy, relations of domination and subordination, and extensive limitations on the individual's freedom to choose.

This does not mean, however, that traditional practices, as such, must be dismantled altogether. Human rights may afford discursive avenues for individual communities and the international community. The human rights regime should be understood in the context of a communicative process. On the one hand, all members of the international community should have equal right to participate in the process of formation of international norms, so that a universal order based on human rights may evolve progressively to accommodate different cultural traditions. On the other hand, if, as discussed above, traditions are ongoing discourse communities, human rights may provide a critical reference point for us to distance ourselves from our own cultural practices and heritage and reflect on them. The idea of human rights may serve to modify, renovate, if not enrich a tradition; it may actually save a tradition instead of destroying it. To refer to a general example, the contemporary discourse on gender equality in many societies may have served to destroy the patriarchal family but not the institution of the family. Instead, it redefines marriage as a relationship between equals, an 'equal partnership'.

Any living tradition is an adaptation to changing objective conditions. Open and rational discourse on human rights may be one of the most important avenues for traditions to adapt themselves to the contemporary world. This assertion is not without material bases. We are no longer living in closed, isolated communities, but in a highly internationalized world with efficient communication processes. There is no one single tradition which is not open to relativization and historicization, challenges and questioning. On the other hand, with the internationalization of the market system, traditional social order based on ascribed roles and hierarchy is no longer effective. The expansion of state functions and bureaucratic control renders individuals powerless and vulnerable, and thus in need of institutional protection against political abuse of power. Most important of all, as Jurgen Habermas states, one of the features distinguishing modern societies from traditional ones is that norms are no longer unquestionably accepted. Instead, the 'legitimation of norms can be met only through appeal to universalistic value systems. . . . 'Today, the only form of universal morality capable of withstanding the destruction of tradition is a communicative ethics in which all politically significant decisions are tied to the formation of rational consensus in unrestricted discourse.'[19]

This is already the kind of communicative ethics that is commonly accepted and recognized as legitimate in international society today. Non-Western and Third World countries in general are demanding equality in participation and dialogue, which is the yardstick to evaluate the legitimacy of international decisions and actions. The core values of autonomy and pluralism are implicit in international politics. In this sense, it is untenable for nations today to argue that human rights values are not part of their culture. It remains for national leaders and governments to be answerable both to their people and to the international community as to why different institutional norms are applied in the conduct of international and domestic politics.

If we accept the idea of tradition as an ongoing discursive process, and grant that liberalism is itself a form of political culture that has always coexisted and worked with other political traditions and community values (in fact, liberalism itself may be an empty, formal doctrine without the presence of substantive community values), there is reason to believe that human rights as derived from Western liberal values can be integrated with Asian community values. In fact, Asian cultures are replete with the ethics of harmony, benevolence, and compassion, ethics that are often the basis of a democratic community. By merging these traditions with the values of freedom, equality, autonomy, and pluralism, Asian cultures may even provide viable alternatives to Western traditions as the bases of political community in the future.

Culture, Ethnicity, and the Politics of Representation — A Critique of the Idea of an 'Asian View of Human Rights'

Implicit in the international human rights regime is equality of participation in dialogues, if not of the capacity to influence and define the terms of discourse. It is not merely based on substantive issues of values that Third World countries often regard human rights as a Western imposition. On issues relating to process and institutions, they regard the inequality of power between superpowers and Third World countries as necessarily putting them on an unequal footing. Western countries have not only defined all the terms of discourse but also utilized their positions of economic and political superiority to pressure weaker parties to comply. Put simply, the human rights regime is viewed as an ideological resource of the 'West' to colonize the 'East'.

In this context, the recent Bangkok Declaration was an attempt by some Asian governments to 'empower' themselves in order to resist such an imposition. The power processes involved in the current human rights dialogue should be an issue of central concern if the ideal is to be truly realized and the legitimacy of the resultant international order commonly accepted. However, one needs also to be critical of the power processes involved in this 'Asian' attempt at empowerment. The Bangkok Declaration, as derived by some Asian political leaders, can be seen as a political construction of 'ethnicity' through the categories of 'East' and 'West'. The construction is a political one in that it imposes a collective identity (Asian/East Asian) on otherwise diverse cultural communities in order to fulfil a political purpose — to create a myth of homogeneity and hence an exclusionary boundary.[20]

The politics of representation here hinges on *who and what truly represent Asia*. The political leaders of the countries concerned claim to represent the views and aspirations of all the peoples in those countries. In reality, political repression has denied many of these peoples the avenues to construct their own narratives and discourses on human rights. Even though the views articulated by these Asian officials are representative of some groups, one has to ask which social groups (such as which class, race, gender, and other minority groups) are being represented and which ones silenced.

On the question of 'what', one needs to ask whether the construction of such an 'Asian view of human rights' serves to naturalize and homogenize cultural practices, and in this process denies their subjects the opportunities for change. Is 'Asia' better represented as one homogeneous group or as diverse cultural communities? Should race, nation, identity, and culture be fixed interest rather than reference points for discourse and reflection? What narrative has been constructed to represent a nation's identity and which others marginalized?[21]

In these senses, the cultural relativist argument implicit in the Bangkok Declaration bears its own negation. Accepting the idea of cultural rights necessarily raises the concern that cultural communities are actually heterogeneous, historical, and dialogical communities. As such, one needs to ask whether the Bangkok Declaration is truly premised on defending cultural interests. As Avtar Brah notes, 'Asia' or the 'East' was historically constructed as the Other as 'Europe' constructed its Self in the process of colonization.[22] It is most ironic that the same cultural resources are now utilized by Asian political leaders to colonize their own people, in the sense of denying them the very cultural right to reflect on their own cultural practices and actively to construct/reconstruct their own identities.

Notes

1. See Alan S. Rosenbaum (ed.), *The Philosophy of Human Rights: International Perspectives*, London: Aldwych Press, 1980, pp. 1–41; James W. Nickel, *Making Sense of Human Rights: Philosophical Reflections on the Universal Declaration of Human Rights*, California: University of California Press, 1987; Alison D. Renteln, *International Human Rights: Universalism Versus Relativism*, Newbury Park, California: Sage Publications, 1990.
2. Rolando Gaete, *Human Rights and the Limits of Critical Reason*, Vermont: Dartmouth Publishing Co., 1993, pp. 4–5.
3. See Jurgen Habermas, *Toward a Rational Society: Student Protest, Science, and Politics*, Translated by Jeremy J. Shapiro, Boston: Beacon Press, 1970, pp. 92–5; Brian Fay, *Social Theory and Political Practice*, New York: Holmes & Meier Publishers, 1975; Thomas McCarthy, *The Critical Theory of Jurgen Habermas* Cambridge: MIT Press, 1981, pp. 16–40.

4. See James W. Nickel, *Making Sense of Human Rights: Philosophical Reflections on the Universal Declaration of Human Rights*, ch. 1–3.
5. For a discussion of the various relativist arguments, see James W. Nickel, *Ibid.*, ch. 4.
6. Alison D. Renteln, *International Human Rights: Universalism Versus Relativism*, p. 11.
7. Hans-Georg Gadamer, 'The Problem of Historical Consciousness,' In Paul Rabinow and William M. Sullivan, eds., *Interpretative Social Science: A Reader*, Berkeley: University of California Press, 1979, p. 108.
8. Jurgen Habermas, 'Review of Gadamer,' pp. 335–6, quoted in Thomas McCarthy, *The Critical Theory of Jurgen Habermas*, p. 171.
9. See Alasdair MacIntyre, *Whose Justice? Which Rationality?*, London: Gerald Duckworth & Co. Ltd., 1988.
10. Richard J. Bernstein, *Beyond Objectivism and Relativism*, Oxford: Basil Blackwell Publisher Ltd., 1983, pp. 79–93.
11. *Ibid*, pp. 93–108.
12. Hans-Georg Gadamer, *Truth and Method*. Translated and edited by Garrett Barden and John Cumming, New York: Seabury Press, 1975. For cursory reading, see Richard J. Bernstein, *Beyond Objectivism and Relativism*, pp. 118–44.
13. See Alasdair MacIntyre, *After Virtue*, Notre Dame, Indiana: University of Notre Dame Press, 1981; Michael Sandel, *Liberalism and the Limits of Justice*, Cambridge: Cambridge University Press, 1982; Charles Taylor, 'Cross-Purposes: The Liberal-Communitarian Debate.' In N. Rosenblum (ed.), *Liberalism and the Moral Life*, Cambridge: Harvard University Press, 1989; Charles Taylor, *Sources of the Self*, Cambridge: Harvard University Press, 1989; Michael Walzer, *Spheres of Justice*, New York: Basic Books, 1983.
14. See John Rawls, *A Theory of Justice*, Cambridge: Harvard University Press, 1971; Robert Nozick, *Anarchy, State and Utopia*, New York: Basic Books, 1974.
15. See Jack Crittenden, *Beyond Individualism, Reconstituting the Liberal Self*, New York: Oxford University Press, 1992.
16. See John Rawls, 'Justice as Fairness: Political not Metaphysical', *Philosophy and Public Affairs*, 14(3), 1985; 'The Priority of Rights and Ideas of the Good,' *Philosophy and Public Affairs*, 17(4), 1988; *Political Liberalism*, New York: Columbia University Press, 1993.
17. Joseph Raz, *The Morality of Freedom*, Oxford: Clarendon Press, 1986; Steven Mulhall, Adam Swift, *Liberals and Communitarians*, 1992.
18. Richard E. Flathman, *The Practice of Rights*, New York: Cambridge University Press, 1976, p. 192.
19. Jurgen Habermas, *Legitimation Crisis*. Translated by Thomas McCarthy, Boston: Beacon Press, 1975. The quotation is from

Thomas McCarthy, *The Critical Theory of Jurgen Habermas*, p. 376.

20. For some discussions of the concept of 'ethnicity,' see Avtar Brah, 'Re-framing Europe: Engendered Racisms, Ethnicities and Nationalisms in Contemporary Western Europe,' *Feminist Review*, 45 (Autumn), 1993; Nira Yuval-Davis, 'Women, Ethnicity and Empowerment,' *Feminism and Psychology*, 4(1), 1994.

21. For some recent discussions on the representation of national identity in Asia and China, see Harumi Befu, ed., *Cultural Nationalism in East Asia: Representation and Identity*, Berkeley: Institute of East Asian Studies, 1993; Edward Friedman, 'Reconstructing China's National Identity: A Southern Alternative to Mao-Era Anti-Imperialist Nationalism,' *The Journal of Asian Studies*, 53(1), 1994; Dru C. Gladney, 'Representing Nationality in China: Refiguring Majority/Minority Identities,' The Journal of Asian Studies 53(1), 1994.

22. Avtar Brah, 'Reframing Europe: En-gendered Racisms, Ethnicities and Nationalisms in Contemporary Western Europe,' p. 10.

Part IV
Contemporary Practices

On Human Rights and Their Guarantee by Law

Yu Haocheng

Although 'human rights' is a topical issue in contemporary international politics, it has been a taboo in our country for a long time. Our record of human rights since 1949 is comparable to that of the former Soviet Union. There have been countless cases of serious violations of human rights. Even the human rights of a former state president, Liu Shaoqi, were not guaranteed. He was publicly condemned; his home was searched and his property confiscated; he was forced to ride 'the jet engine' (a Red Guard practice of forcing one into a humiliating position with arms extended and head forced down); he was kicked and beaten and sent to jail illegally. He met a miserable death in prison only after suffering a long period of torture.

Nevertheless, both before and during the Cultural Revolution in the 1960s and 1970s, some of our countrymen just closed their eyes and denied what was happening, both with respect to Liu and countless other examples of abuse. They said there was no problem of human rights in our country, using the phrase 'imperialist states' interference in our country's internal affairs' to fend off all external criticisms.

Chinese nationals who wrote about their country's human rights were denounced as 'the yes-men of imperialism'. In 1979 there emerged many essays attacking the notion of human rights, claiming that 'human rights' is 'no slogan of the proletariat', but belongs rather to the bourgeoisie. Then in 1983 a wave of anti-humanitarianism arose. Nearly all words related to 'human' — human nature, human integrity, human rights, and humanitarianism, etc. — were labelled as bourgeois and severely censured.

This criticism was reflected in a report in the *World Economic Herald* about an interview with the writer Xia Yan, a former Deputy Minister of Culture who was himself persecuted during the Cultural Revolution:

> The revered Mr Xia has his own ideas on matters related to 'Man'. He points out that socialist countries do not care

about human rights. Under socialism anything to do with
'Man', such as human rights, human nature, human integrity and humanitarianism, etc., is considered a taboo. He
gave the example of Zhou Yang, a writer who was criticized for talking about humanitarianism. Under such views
even creative self-expression was penalized. Hence Reagan
used this deficiency in dealing with Gorbachev. Xia asked
whether this might call for some reflection on our part.
Now the leadership suggest that we should focus on the
development of productivity. Xia complains that the most
revolutionary and dynamic forces behind productivity —
human beings — have long been neglected by us. This he
feels has led to many problems.[1]

At the United Nations and international conferences, our
country's representatives have always shied away from any
discussion of human rights. They seemed to have neither the
confidence nor the conscience to assert themselves, falling
instead into a passive position. There are welcome signs that
this situation has changed somewhat in recent years.

Our statesmen have finally learned that the issue of human
rights cannot be avoided in international settings. If you do
not talk about your own country's record, others will. Human
rights are not the monopoly of Western countries. So, on
the one hand, our country's leaders have instructed the relevant departments to start researching the theories of human
rights. As a result, government documents, like the *White
Paper on Human Rights in China* (November 1991), *China's
Reformed Criminals* (August 1992), and *Tibet's Sovereignty and
Human Rights* (September 1992), were successively promulgated.[2] On the other hand, our leaders abandoned the 'ostrich
policy' they had all along pursued on the international stage
and started having dialogues on the issue of human rights
with the international community.

Since then more and more essays on human rights have
appeared and books on this topic have also been published
in China. Notwithstanding that some were still 'deferential'
works saturated with slogans similar to those of the 'Cultural
Revolution' — which are shallow, arbitrary, trite, and could
simply be ignored — some were indeed based on the research
results of scholars who had broken through the barrier to
adopt an objective and independent attitude towards the
research and theories of their overseas counterparts. The
latter readings can open people's minds.

Here I will try to express my views on the few points of dispute regarding the issue of human rights in our country. I will, in particular, focus on their guarantee by law. I hope this will help scholars here and abroad, and readers in general, to grasp the issue better.

Debates on the Theory of Human Rights

The Universality and Class Nature of Human Rights

From a Marxist point of view, things in a class society, like democracy and freedom, have a class nature. Human rights are of course no exception. The point is, when we affirm the class nature of human rights, we should not, at the same time, refute their universality. In the essay 'The Protection of Human Rights is Correct and Conducive to the Progress of the Human Race — Commemorating the 40th Anniversary of the Universal Declaration of Human Rights,' (1988), I wrote:

> What are human rights? Human rights are the rights of human beings. They eliminate all discrimination in terms of nation, race, religion, nationality, sex, age, and especially, class. They embrace all human beings and are universal. Hence Marx and Engels described human rights as 'the most common type of rights'. Likewise, some people often quoted the following part from Mao Zedong's 'Speech at the Yenan Art and Cultural Seminar' to support their arguments: 'Is there a thing called "human nature"? Of course there is. But there is only a concrete human nature, no human nature in the abstract. In a class society there is merely a "class human nature" and no human nature which transcends class divisions'. In fact, Mao, in a letter to Lei Jingtian dated as early as October 10, 1937, said that the gunning-down of Liu Qian by Huang Kegong was 'an act which betrayed the principle of the party, the cause of the revolution and the principle of "man as man"'. Through this he asserted the existence of a universal human nature. I think the same universality should be applied to human rights.[3]

Some people have fiercely attacked my view that 'human rights are the rights of human beings' stated above, regarding this kind of 'abstract human rights' as a departure from Marxism. They have gone so far as to quote these words to demonstrate 'the rampant advance of the notions of bourgeois democracy, liberty (including the so-called absolute freedom of creative expression in art and culture) and human rights (accusing some of even making theoretical arguments) in the last ten years'; and have charged that this proved that the various propaganda on human rights not only has a market but quite a stirring social effect in our circle of literary and cultural theorists. Nonetheless, until now I still maintain that there is nothing wrong with my statement.

On 1 June 1945, forty-eight countries (including China — the representative of the then 'China Liberated Zone', Dong Biwu, was in the delegation) signed the Charter of the United Nations. Article 1(3) of the Charter listed the purposes and principles as follows: 'To achieve international cooperation in solving international problems of an economic, social, cultural, and humanitarian character and in promoting and encouraging respect for human rights and for fundamental freedoms for all without distinction as to race, sex, language or religion.'[4]

In December 1948, the United Nations passed the Universal Declaration of Human Rights. Article 1 states, 'All human beings are born free and equal in dignity and rights'; and Article 2 states, 'Everyone is entitled to all the rights and freedoms set forth in this Declaration, without distinction of any kind, such as race, color, sex, language, religion, political or other opinions, national or social origin, property, birth or other status.'[5]

All the above concern the universality of human rights. In December 1988, when our country's representative to the United Nations, Ding Yuanhong, gave a speech on behalf of our government at a ceremony commemorating the fortieth anniversary of the Universal Declaration of Human Rights, he affirmed the content of the Charter of the United Nations and the Universal Declaration of Human Rights, as follows:

> The Chinese government and people have all along advocated respect for human rights and fundamental freedoms. We have supported and abided by the principles relating to human rights enshrined in the Charter of the United Nations. We have also actively participated in many UN activities in the area of human rights. China has entered into a series of international agreements on human rights, carried out the duties under them conscientiously and submitted on time reports to the relevant supervisory bodies. Now, as we commemorate the fortieth anniversary of the

'Declaration', our country, like others, has launched its own commemorative activities. We believe these activities will encourage governments and peoples all over the world to adhere to the aims of the Charter and the principles laid down in other international agreements on human rights, raise the level of human rights enjoyed by all peoples and make positive contributions towards the safeguarding of world peace and justice.[6]

I would like to point out that, contrary to the above self-congratulatory statement, the stress on the class nature of human rights at the expense of their universality has led to serious consequences for the protection of human rights in our country. In all previous political upheavals, there was always a group of people who were perceived as 'hostile elements' (in each movement, there was different labels, such as the Hu-Feng gang, capitalist rightists, capitalist roaders, anti-revolutionary revisionists, bourgeois liberalists, turmoil leaders, etc.) and had some of their civil rights taken away simply because their political views were different from those of the Party and the Government. These deprivations were clearly acts which violated human rights and went against the principles of the Universal Declaration of Human Rights.

I agree with the following scholarly opinions. Sun Zhe argues:

> Analyzing the issue of human rights from the class angle is both necessary and correct. But this is not the only one way which excludes all others. We must be brave and admit that the struggle for human rights has facilitated economic development and political progress in capitalist society. Besides, not only the ruling class benefits. For example, the social welfare systems of most Western societies are aimed at those being ruled. Their content, such as compulsory education, the protection of children and the conservation of the environment and the ecosystem, etc., are also welcomed by their recipients. From lessons in history, we must overcome the absolutist and superficial way of thinking when we reflect on the class nature of human rights. After all, class nature is but one, rather than the only, attribute of human rights.[7]

Xia Yong pointed out correctly that Marx never refuted that human rights were abstract and universal. Xia said:

> There are two sides to the concept of human rights: one normative and the other empirical, i.e., a distinction between what ought to be and what is. Generally speaking, the

concept of human rights is applied in a normative manner to express people's desire for a certain ideal situation. A more popular definition of human rights is, 'Claims asserted as those which should be, or sometimes stated to be those which are, legally recognized and protected to secure for each individual the fullest and freest development of personality and spiritual, moral and other independence' (reference to the *Oxford Companion to Law*). These rights belong to everybody, 'without distinction as to race, colour, sex, language, religion, political or other opinion, national or social origin, property, birth or other status' (Universal Declaration of Human Rights). Clearly, human rights are firstly a kind of moral right. They require the acknowledgement, protection, and promotion of the interests and demands entitled to man as man.

According to this definition, human rights are the rights to which you are entitled, as long as you are a human being. In other words, so long as you are a human being, you are entitled to have certain interests and demands protected. Such rights, interests, or demands are usually interpreted as liberty, equality, security, and the pursuit of happiness.

These demands, as expounded in the concept of human rights, are the common needs of all human beings. Ideas and thoughts expressing such needs in various degrees and ways were present in all ages and civilizations. Whether such needs could become the demand for individual rights, or whether a secular concept of right could arise from the moral thoughts incorporating such needs would depend on history, civilization, tradition, and social development.[8]

Xia continued with his analysis of Marx's views as follows:

Whether one starts from the logic of the thoughts of the whole human race or that of modern Western thought, obviously what Marx criticized was not the normative human rights, but the practice of human rights in real life. Marx did not criticize people's demands for human rights; what he disapproved of were existing institutions of human rights or those waving the banner of human rights. Marx considered the modern institutions of human rights in the West a sham, showing clearly that there was in his mind a better concept of human rights which was true and reasonable. If he was not seeking the truth and the best, why did he condemn falsehood and narrowness? Hence it is very dangerous to regard Marx's empirical evaluation of human rights as his whole concept of human rights, in the same way as one should not turn Marx's empirical evaluations of 'state' and 'law' as 'expressing the consciousness of the ruling class' into a normative one. Popular views such as 'human rights could not be applied in China' and 'human rights are but a way of the bourgeoisie in the West', etc., are examples of such a danger.[9]

I think there is some wisdom in the above points of view. We should bear them in mind when we discuss the class and universal nature of human rights.

The Contents of Human Rights

The umbrella 'human rights' encompasses a wide range of rights. They can be divided into four categories: the right to life, economic rights, political rights, and cultural rights. Internationally, human rights are usually divided into two groups: (i) civil and political rights, and (ii) economic, social, and cultural rights. Although scholars have different views on the contents and classification of human rights, their main point of contention is the relationship between (i) and (ii), i.e., whether the two groups of rights should have equal weight or which one, political or social rights, should have priority over the other.

Some books and pamphlets on human rights have quoted Article 13 of the 'Teheran Proclamation' passed by the World Human Rights Conference held in Teheran on 13 May 1968: 'Human rights and fundamental freedoms cannot be separated. If there are no economic, social and cultural rights; civil and political rights can never be realized.' In the words of John Humphrey, a human rights expert and the United Nations' first human rights secretary, in 'The Manifesto of Mankind', 'Human rights based on empty belief are nearly meaningless.'[10]

People have often heard arguments like this: democracy cannot feed people, i.e., freedom of speech is meaningless for one with an empty stomach or a man who cannot afford to go to school. As subsistence is primary, so social rights are more important than political rights. Such arguments may sound convincing but are in fact specious and cannot withstand close scrutiny. The above suggestions clearly demonstrate the degree of confusion in defining human rights today.

David D. Raphael divided rights into two types: rights of action and rights of recipience.[11] The former are negative and the latter positive. The former only require the agent not to obstruct, i.e., one should have the right to act according to his wishes without others' interference (i.e. negative freedom). The latter are rights which can only be established and exercised through certain acts of an agent (positive freedom).

For example, enshrined in the thirty articles of the Universal Declaration on Human Rights passed by the United Nations General Assembly in 1948 are rights which could clearly be put into two categories; a) primitive or political rights, such as the right of free speech, of assembly, and of movement, etc., which can be exercised so long as public authorities (state and government) acknowledge their legality and do not obstruct them; b) extended rights, such as the right of receiving education and basic social welfare, etc., whose exercise requires positive participation and the provision of certain material conditions by public authorities, that is social rights.[12]

A common description of the word 'right' is 'what one can do' and this refers to political rights. In contrast, social rights refer to 'what one should receive'. The two are clearly not the same thing. For example, the meaning of the right of speech is obvious, i.e., a person can express his opinions and no one can interfere with him. However, what is the right to education? There are at least two meanings: a) nobody can forbid another person from going to school on whatever grounds; and b) each child is entitled to go to school even though he or she may not be able to afford the fee or pass the examination. Clearly the former accords with the original meaning of 'right', whilst the latter is more a welfare issue.

Albert Einstein, in his discussion on liberty, quoted many times a sentence from Arthur Schopenhauer: 'A man can do as he will, but not will as he will'.[13] We know that the concept of human rights originates from the theories of natural law, which deal with what one has under the state of nature. For example, Robinson Crusoe, marooned on a desert island, could still talk and search for food freely. Although he was free from others' interference he might not have had enough to eat or the necessary treatment when he fell ill. The case of Crusoe clearly demonstrates what are and what are not rights: he could do as he liked, but he might not get all he wanted.

From this we can draw the conclusion that rights have a

priority over welfare, or political rights take precedence over social rights (if one insists they must be called rights). When we evaluate a government, we must first of all look at whether it has infringed upon the fundamental rights (i.e., negative freedom or political rights) of its citizens. We then proceed to examine whether it has provided enough welfare to it citizens. When talking about welfare, we must not forget that a government is, after all, a power rather than a productive institution. Hence it is wrong to say for example, that a government has fed its people.

As mentioned above, according to Raphael's categorization of human rights, social rights are rights of recipience, which can only be established and exercised through certain positive acts of the agent. But the body and content of social rights have not been ascertained. Hence the various economic, cultural, and social rights enshrined in the Universal Declaration of Human Rights are actually normative rights shrouded in idealism. On the other hand, political rights are empirical rights immediately realizable so long as the government does not interfere. So the distinction is apparent. Hence the view that 'political rights are but a luxury when people are still hungry' is really absurd.

Such views are, in fact, pretty trite. Luo Longji, a renowned democrat from our country, as early as 1929, wrote the following in the essay 'On Human Rights':

> Those who have gone bankrupt in human rights cheat themselves by saying that 'human rights' is an abstract term, a pet phrase one can neither eat when hungry nor wear when cold. So, the human rights movement is not as practical as the materialistic class revolution. Basically these people have not thought about what human rights are. Of course human rights include clothing, food and many other things more important than these two. To put it naughtily, if there were absolute freedoms of thought, speech and press in Germany in Marx's days, he would not have had to take refuge in a London antique shop to write his *Das Kapital*.[14]

The results of the 25 April 1993 plebiscite in Russia also showed that despite some economic difficulties on the way to reform, the Russians still supported political reform and no longer wanted to return to the Stalinist style of totalitarian rule. The plebiscite results strongly refute the ridiculous argument of 'democracy cannot fill one's stomach'.

The Relationship Between Human Rights and Sovereignty

Do human rights take precedence over sovereignty or vice versa? This is hotly debated both within and outside the country. Apart from some propagandist essays and pamphlets which still insist that 'human rights are a country's internal affairs, which other countries cannot interfere with', and level typical critiques on such ideas as that 'human rights are boundless'; 'humanitarianism cannot be tampered with', 'limited sovereignty' and 'the concept of sovereignty is anachronistic', etc., some scholars have adopted a compromising and non-confrontational approach. The following statements are illustrative:

> On this issue, our government's consistent position is: generally speaking, human rights are within the limits of national law and can only be exercised under national law. Other countries and international bodies have no right to interfere with them. But for some special cases, which have actually gone beyond national boundaries, we should, on the one hand, maintain the principle of national sovereignty and fight against attempts to use human rights as an excuse to blow up the issue and interfere with the internal affairs of another country. On the other hand, we should accept the fact that the protection of human rights has already entered the sphere of international law, and that such protection is progressive and reasonable and we should support a certain degree of international intervention.[15]

It seems that some Chinese scholars do not agree with the idea of categorizing human rights entirely as an internal affair. They think there can be some exceptions. The international law of human rights is outside the arena of internal affairs. On the one hand, no country can use whatever excuse or tactic to interfere with another country's internal affairs. Likewise no country can use internal affairs as an excuse to contravene the principles of international law or refrain from carrying out its obligations on human rights protection under international agreements.[16]

However, there is still an ongoing debate among Chinese scholars about which human rights are within or outside the sphere of internal affairs and which rights should be protected under international law. In fact, with the development of international law, fundamental human rights have already been embodied in international law, and the sphere of national jurisdiction is diminishing. This allows international supervision and condemnation, or even sanction, against a country whose record of internal human rights is not up to standard. Apartheid, racial discrimination, ethnic cleansing, slavery, terrorist acts, torture, discrimination, and abuse against women, children, and the handicapped, etc., have in general been accepted as matters to be protected by international law.

The biggest dispute at present is whether the violation of civil and political rights can be put into this category. One view is that the protection of human rights is the main responsibility of a sovereign power and hence it is entirely a matter of internal affairs. The inadequacy of this view is that it cannot provide a reasonable and satisfactory answer to the following question: If it is the sovereign government which infringes upon or tramples the human rights of its citizens, what is to be done? From the standpoint of those who support absolute sovereignty, one could only look on when a regime cruelly abused and tortured its citizens, and all resolutions safeguarding human rights passed by the United Nations amount to mere scraps of paper.

The scenario was succinctly put by British legal scholar on international law, Hersch Lauterpacht: 'None of the essential objects of international organizations can be secured without the surrender of what are often regarded as vital attributes of the sovereignty of States in the international sphere.'[17] National sovereignty should, therefore, not be absolute and limitless, but relative and bounded. Absolute sovereignty can only negate the order of international law.

For example, when a military regime refuses to hand over power to a democratic party returned by a lawful election but puts the party's leader in jail, international supervision, intervention, and sanctions are clearly necessary. And when the United Nations passed resolutions to send peace-keeping troops to protect the Kurdish minorities in Iraq and the Somalis who were dying from the onslaught of armed bandits, hunger, and cold, such humanitarian and righteous acts could hardly be dismissed as 'intervention in another country's internal affairs' or 'imperialist aggression'.

The same rationale applies when your neighbour is killing his sons and daughters. You cannot possibly just sit there and pretend that you have not heard any call for help. According to the principles of 'the interests of citizens are above all' and 'the supreme citizen', the answer to whether sovereignty takes precedence over human rights or vice versa is obvious.

The crux of the matter is: the State should exist for the interests of its citizens and not the other way round. As Albert Einstein has said in the essay 'The Limits of Sovereignty':

> 'The state is built for the people, but the people do not live for the state. . . . Whoever holds the view that the individual is the most supreme in Man agrees with this. . . . I think the most important mission of a country is to protect individuals so as to turn them into creative people . . . . The state should be our servant, and we should not be the slaves of the state.'[18]

Here we should also make a fine distinction between patriotism and statism. Statism is often sham patriotism. One must first love one's countrymen before one can claim to be patriotic. We should bear in mind the people's liberty and happiness when we consider all matters. Moreover, the State and government are not the same thing. The torture, infringement, and trampling of human rights in the name of the State by a government should not be allowed. In this respect it is important to consider what China's actual practice is in respect of human rights, the laws, and their enforcement.

The Guarantee of Human Rights by Law

Human rights are generally expressed as the civil rights prescribed by the State and its legal regulations. But the concept of human rights is different from that of civil rights. Civil rights are political rights, i.e., what Marx described as rights 'which can only be exercised if one is a member of a community. Their content is participation in community life, in the political life of the community, the life of the state. They fall in the category of political liberty, of civil rights.'[19]

Another part of human rights, i.e., those human rights outside the sphere of civil rights, are expressed as 'natural rights'. From the bourgeois-democratic revolution in the eighteenth century onward, many countries have followed in the footsteps of the United States and France to lay down in their constitutions the fundamental rights of their citizens. Relevant laws safeguarding such rights have also been formulated.

As for our country, our constitutions, from the first constitution in 1954 to the present one drawn up in 1982, all contain a chapter on 'The Fundamental Rights and Duties of Citizens' prescribing the various freedoms and rights to which citizens are entitled. Our country's human rights situation and in particular the protection of civil and political rights, as well as the safeguarding of human rights in our judicial process, have all been discussed in the White Paper on Human Rights in China issued by the State Council's Information Bureau in October 1991.

However, when we explore in depth our country's record on human rights and compare it with other countries, we cannot deny that there is still much room for improvement. One problem is that the freedoms and rights to which some citizens are entitled are not yet written into the constitution. Secondly, even those already in the constitution cannot be guaranteed without complementary legal provisions. There are cases of total disregard for the law and lax enforcement. As a result, Chinese citizens cannot exercise some legal rights at all. The following is an analysis of the obstacles to the protection of human rights in our country.

Personal Liberty

Our present constitution states that the personal liberty of a citizen is inviolable. Depriving or restricting the personal liberty of a citizen by illegal imprisonment or other illicit means is not allowed. Article 2 of the Law on Arrest and Detention of the People's Republic of China stipulates that citizens 'cannot be arrested without the verdict of the people's court or the approval of the people's procuratorate'.

But in actual life such protection of personal liberty is not afforded. The measure of 'shelter and investigation' (*shourong shencha*) is often adopted, allowing public security bodies to arrest citizens arbitrarily, although '*shourong shencha*' has never been defined in law. As an administrative penalty, 're-education/rehabilitation through labour' (*laodong jiaoyang*) has practically restricted, if not deprived, the personal freedom of those being re-educated. So it is an administrative body (the Re-education Through Labour Management Committee), instead of the courts, which rules on whether a citizen's personal liberty should be removed.

This practice does not conform with the spirit of a number of international agreements. Under Article 3 of the Universal Declaration of Human Rights, 'Everyone has the right to life, liberty and the security of person'; Article 9 states, 'No one shall be subjected to arbitrary arrest, detention or exile'. Under Article 8 of the International Covenant on Civil and Political Rights, 'No one shall be held in slavery or servitude'; Article 9 states, 'No one shall be deprived of his liberty except on such grounds and in accordance with such procedures as are established by law.'

As a coercive measure under the Law on Criminal Litigation of the People's Republic of China, 'supervision at home' (*jianshi juzhu*) is defined as 'supervision at home by the local police station and the section of the people's commune in charge of the defendant's unit delegated with the task'. Instead of depriving the defendant completely of his personal liberty, this legal provision only restricts his activity to an area such as his home where he is watched. But in practice the defendant is often taken to other places where he is literally detained and his personal liberty tightly restricted, if not removed altogether. Article 92 of this law stipulates, 'A defendant cannot be detained for more than two months during investigation. In complicated situations where the case has not been closed before the deadline, the people's procuratorate at a higher level can extend the deadline by one month.' However, the deadline is seldom met and detention may last for years.

In addition, the policy of 'staying to work after serving one's sentence' (*liuchang jiuye*), which our country has carried out for years, means that a defendant may not have his personal liberty restored even after he has served his sentence. This is quite the opposite of the guarantee of personal liberty by legal provisions.

Freedom of Thought

Before our country was established in 1949, leaders of the Chinese Communist Party had made some human rights provisions in various parts of the country, such as the 'Regulations on the Guarantee of Human and Property Rights in the Border Areas of Shanxi, Gansu and Ningxia' and the 'Regulations on the Guarantee of Human Rights in Northwest Shanxi'.

Both stipulated that all citizens have 'freedom of thought and religion'.[20] In Mao's works it is often mentioned that human rights should include freedom of thought. For example, in 'On Policy', Mao said, 'It should be stipulated that those who do not oppose the resistance against Japan — landlords, capitalist, workers and peasants — are to have equal human rights, property rights, voting rights and the freedom of speech, assembly, association, thought and religion.'[21]

And in 'On Coalition Government', he wrote, 'The citizens' freedom of speech, publication, assembly, association, thought, religion and personal liberty are the most important types of freedom.'[22] The 'Common Guidelines of the Chinese People's Political Consultative Conference', which served as a temporary constitution when our country was newly established, also had provisions concerning freedom of thought. Article 5 stated, 'The citizens of the People's Republic of China have the freedoms of thought, speech, publication, assembly, association, correspondence, residence, movement, religion, demonstration, protest and personal liberty.'[23]

But since the 1954 Constitution, freedom of thought has disappeared. The freedom of belief, which refers only to religious belief and not to belief in any ideology, remains. Then in 1975, 'Marxism, Leninism and Maozedong Thought' were written into the constitution as 'the theoretical basis of the guiding thoughts of our country'; Article 11 provides, 'State apparatus and personnel must conscientiously study Marxism, Leninism and Maozedong Thought' (The state apparatus is not a human being. How can it learn any ideology? Even the sentence is incomprehensible. How ridiculous!). Although this article was deleted from the 1978 Constitution, 'Marxism, Leninism and Maozedong Thought' were included in the Preamble: 'All the revolutionary and infrastructural successes of our country result from the guidance of Marxism, Leninism and Maozedong Thought.' The so-called 'Four Cardinal Principles' were added to the Preamble of the 1982 Constitution as follows: 'Under the leadership of the Communist Party of China and the guidance of Marxism–Leninism and Maozedong Thought, the Chinese people of all nationalities will continue to adhere to the people's democratic dictatorship and follow the socialist road . . . to turn China into a socialist country with a high level of culture and democracy.'

Some legal experts in our country concluded from this that

'the Four Cardinal principles have been written into the constitution' and 'the constitution's preamble has legal effect'. Does this arbitrary inclusion of an ideology into the law not go against the principle of the freedom of thought? Four hundred years ago, the Italian philosopher Bruno said, 'The state has no right to tell its citizens what to think.' In the Han Dynasty, Emperor Wu banned the 'hundred schools of thought' (a reference to the large number of philosophical schools contending at that time) and adopted that of Confucius only, putting to an end the 'contention of a hundred schools of thought' between the Spring and Autumn and Warring States periods. This had enormous negative repercussions on the historical development of thought in our country.

Lin Biao claimed at the beginning of the 'Cultural Revolution' that 'there should be a united thought for our country's 700 million citizens, and it should be Maozedong Thought.' Such attempts to turn an ideology into a state doctrine are no different from the notion of 'One ideology, One party, and One leader' advocated by Guomindang fascists; they also run counter to the letter and spirit of Article 18 of the Universal Declaration of Human Rights: 'Everyone has the right to freedom of thought, conscience and religion.'

Freedom of Speech, Publication, and Participation in Academic, Artistic, and Cultural Activities

Our country's successive constitutions have all stipulated that citizens have freedom of speech. However, Article 51 of the present constitution says, 'The exercise by citizens of the People's Republic of China of their freedoms and rights may not infringe upon the interests of the state, of society and of the collective, or upon the lawful freedoms and rights of other citizens.' Since our country still does not have any law on news and publication specifying what kind of speech is forbidden, and the crime of counter-revolutionary incitement is not defined in detail in Article 102 of the Law on Criminal Litigation, citizens' freedom of speech and publication can be arbitrarily restricted or removed whenever they are considered 'damaging to the interests of the state, the society or the collective'.

The mass media have all along been perceived as 'the mouth-piece of the party'. There is still a ban on unofficial publications. Under these circumstances, political thoughts and opinions which are different from those of the ruling party and the government hardly have any chance of expression, and the authors of literary and academic works are often denied the right to defend themselves. Information disseminated through the press, the radio, and the television have all been distilled. Newspapers and periodicals imported from Hong Kong, Macau, Taiwan, and further abroad are strictly censored or embargoed. The citizens' right to know (or understand) is severely restricted and people often have to wait for news already exported abroad to travel back to China to get a grip on what really happened in their own country.

One cannot deny that this is a long way from what is stipulated in Article 19 of the Universal Declaration of Human Rights: 'Everyone has the right to freedom of opinion and expression; this right includes freedom to hold opinions without interference and to seek, receive and impart information and ideas through any medium and regardless of frontiers.'

Freedom of Association

Successive constitutions of our country have asserted that citizens have the freedom of association, but so far there is no relevant law. There is only an administrative rule promulgated by the State Council, the Regulation on the Registration and Management of Social Organizations, which refers to social rather than political organizations or parties.

There is also no law pertaining to political parties. The words 'political party' appear in the Preamble and Article 5 of our constitution, but there is no mention of who they are. Apart from the Chinese Communist Party, it seems fair to conclude that only the eight democratic parties which have been participating in the Chinese People's Political Consultative Conference since 1949 are lawful.

Although the law does not say whether it will be lawful to set up new political parties, this is actually forbidden. The Law on the Registration and Management of Social Organizations stipulates that one must first apply and get approval from a civil department before one can set up a social organization. This provision literally puts all social organizations under the government's control. Their leaders are often party or government officials or are appointed by such. So they become 'official' or 'semi-official' organizations.

For example, although many members of the Union of Chinese Writers are dissatisfied with its leadership, they have no right to form a separate organization. Workers' activities in forming free unions were also banned after the lesson of the Polish Solidarity Party. Hence there seems to be a gulf between the legal and actual freedom of association. We have a long way to go before social organizations can act on behalf of the society as independent political forces to scrutinize the activities of the party and the government.

Freedom of Residence and Movement

There was a provision on freedom of residence and movement in our country's first constitution, the one promulgated in 1954. But this was removed in the three successive constitutions. Our country strictly controls the movement of the rural population into the urban areas. Urban and rural populations are not accorded the same treatment. Moreover, the freedom of entering and leaving the country should naturally be a right of every citizen, but this is also severely restricted in our country.

Article 13 of the Universal Declaration of Human Rights provides that, 'Everyone has the right to freedom of movement and residence within the borders of each state; everyone has the right to leave any country, including his own, and to return to his country.' It is plain to see that a big gap still exists in this respect between our country's situation and the standard of human rights recognized by the international community.

Freedom to Strike

The 1954 Constitution contained no mention of the freedom to strike, which was later laid down in the 1975 and 1978 Constitutions. In the Report on the Amendment of the Constitution issued in January 1975, Zhang Chunqiao, a member of the now infamous 'Gang of Four' (this group, with the participation of Mao's wife, led the leftist forces during the most extreme period of the Cultural Revolution), claimed that the inclusion of the citizens' freedom to strike was 'based on Chairman Mao's suggestion'. But this provision was removed again in the 1982 Constitution. The reason, according to a legal expert who participated in the drafting process, was that under the socialist system, 'workers are the masters of the state. The interests of workers and the state are the same. A strike can only jeopardize the interests of the state and the workers themselves, damaging the economy and social order and bringing inconvenience to the work and lives of the people.'[24]

This is an example of asking citizens to sacrifice the interests they are entitled to for those of the state, the society, and the collective. However, the situation has changed a lot as private enterprise and foreign investment have become more and more important in our economy. Even if there were a kernel of truth in the reasons given above, they are no longer sound.

The Principle of the Presumption of Innocence Before Conviction

This principle is generally adopted by the judiciary in most countries of the world. As early as 200 years ago, in August 1789, France promulgated the Declaration of the Rights of Man, of which Article 9 provides, 'Anyone not yet convicted is presumed to be innocent.'[25] Under Clause 1 of Article 11 of the Universal Declaration of Human Rights, 'Everyone charged with a penal offence has the right to be presumed innocent until proved guilty according to law in an open trial.'

Before 1957, most legal scholars in our country agreed with this principle. During the anti-rightist movement, however, it was viewed as a bourgeois argument 'beneficial to the defendant', and many legal scholars were criticized and denounced as 'rightists' for upholding this principle. Since the Third Plenum of the Eleventh Central Committee of the Chinese Communist Party, all legal points condemned in 1957 have been reinstated. The only exception is the presumption of innocence. In the 'anti-spiritual pollution' campaign starting in late 1981 (and continuing off and on until the present), the presumption of innocence was again denounced as a bourgeois legal point of view, creating a wave of anxiety among those who had openly supported the principle in their essays.

The official line is, the Chinese judiciary follows the principle of adhering to facts and the law in its investigations and trials. A criminal suspect is presumed to be neither guilty nor innocent but tried by law in accordance with the facts.[26] But this policy of seeking truth from facts is no substitute for the presumption of innocence since the crux of the matter is: What is the legal status of the defendant before the facts have been dug out and the court has given its verdict?

Here is a case in point: On 31 March 1993, *The Legal System Daily* reported that people were at loggerheads for five months on the proper investigation procedures to follow after a 15-year-old girl in a Tuanzhou high school (in Hunan Province) committed suicide. The report sparked off debates over the proper way of investigating accusations of student misbehaviour. The girl had been interrogated several times in one night and ordered to 'expose' her books and other belongings. Although there was no evidence to indicate that she had stolen money, the school authority maintained that she had not been proved innocent. The case demonstrated vividly that it is necessary and correct that the presumption of innocence be exercised to protect human rights.

I am delighted to see that 'the presumption of innocence' clause has already been written into the Basic Law of the Hong Kong Special Administrative Region passed by the Third Plenum of the Seventh National People's Congress in April 1990. Article 87 provides, 'Anyone who is lawfully arrested shall have the right to a fair trial by the judicial organs without delay and shall be presumed innocent until convicted by the judicial organs.' Now we must ask when will this 'capitalist' legal provision used in Hong Kong be equally applicable on the 'socialist' mainland.

It is absurd to dismiss as 'bourgeois' the principle of 'the presumption of innocence' and to reject it altogether. This principle, like democracy, liberty, and equality before the law, is the product of the anti-feudalist democratic revolution brought about by the historical unity of the bourgeoisie, the proletariat, and the masses. They are the mutual achievements of the progress of human civilization. If the principle of 'presumption of innocence' is written into the constitution and relevant laws, this will not only help safeguard human rights but also lead to fewer unjust charges.

Unenforcable Supervision

Our present constitution states that its implementation is to be supervised by the National People's Congress and its Standing Committees instead of a special body. This, in fact, means no one is overseeing the implementation of the constitution. The job of supervision should include the examination of all laws and regulations to find out if they are constitutional. The National People's Congress and its Standing Committees clearly cannot sufficiently review laws passed by themselves. As no other body is responsible for this, citizens cannot seek legal redress for any unconstitutional acts by the state apparatus and leaders. Are those laws, regulations, and operating details which mean to guarantee the rights of citizens totally constitutional in letter and in spirit? People are very concerned about this. Hence it is essential that an authoritative body be set up to examine the constitutionality of our laws.

Conclusion

Since the Third Plenum of the Eleventh Central Committee of the Chinese Communist Party, we have achieved a lot in strengthening our socialist democracy and our legal system and safeguarding the freedom and rights of our citizens. However, there are many inadequacies, some very serious. Any fundamental improvements in human rights in our country must be accompanied by ongoing political reform, the development of socialist democracy, and the perfection of our legal system. The improvement of our human rights situation is not only necessary for building a democratic, civilized, strong, and prosperous modern state, it is also a step forward for all of humanity.

Notes

(Most sources are Chinese and titles are translated)
1. *World Economic Herald*, (Shijie Jingji Daobao), 20 June 1988, p. 16.
2. *Human Rights in China*, Beijing: Information Office of the State Council, 1991; *China's Reformed Criminals*, Beijing: Information

Office of the State Council, 1992; *Tibet's Sovereignty and Human Rights*, Beijing: Information Office of the State Council, 1992.

3. See, *World Knowledge*, Beijing: World Knowledge Press (Shijie Zhishi Chubanshe), 1988, Vol. 23. Lei Jingtian, the addressee of Mao's letter, was the then presiding judge of the Supreme Court of the border area of Shanxi, Gansu, and Ningxia. Huang Kegong joined the Red Army at an early age and took part in the War of Jinggangshan and the 25,000-mile Long March. He was later the captain of Team Six of the Anti-Japanese Military and Political University. Huang killed Liu Qian, a student of North Shanxi Public School, in October 1937 for turning down his marriage proposal. A public trial was held in the Supreme Court of the border area of Shanxi, Gansu, and Ningxia, and Huang was sentenced to death.

4. Charter of the United Nations, 26 June 1945, *Y.B.U.N.*, 1976: 1043, Article 1(3).

5. Universal Declaration of Human Rights, 10 December 1948, U.N. G.A. Res. 217 A (III), U.N. Doc. A/810, at 71 (1948).

6. Ding Yuanhang speech, *World Knowledge*, Beijing: World Knowledge Press (Shijie Zhi Chubanshe), 1988, Vol. 24.

7. Sun Zhe, *On a New Theory of Human Rights*, Henan: Henan People's Press (Henan Remin Chubanshe), 1992, pp. 61–62, 70.

8. Xia Yong, *The Origin of the Concept of Human Rights*, Beijing: Chinese University of Politics and Law Press (Zhongguo Zhengfa Daxue Chubanshe), 1992, p. 199.

9. *Ibid*, p. 200.

10. Pang Sen, *The ABCs of Human Rights Today*, Sichuan: Sichuan People's Press (Sichuan Renmin Chubanshe), 1991, pp. 26–27.

11. David D. Raphael, *Problems of Political Philosophy*, London: MacMillan Press, 1970, pp. 68–70.

12. Lin Jia, *A Hundred Questions and Answers on Human Rights*, Beijing: World Knowledge Press (Shijie Zhishi Chubanshe), 1992, pp. 22–23.

13. Albert Einstein, *The Essays of Einstein*, Chinese Edition, Beijing: Commercial Press (Shangwu Yinshu Guan), 1979, Part III, p. 42, see also *The World as I See It*, New York: Philosophical Library, 1949, p. 2.

14. First appeared in Luo Longji, *Political Theses*, New Moon Book Store (Xin Yue Shu Dian), January 1932.

15. Sun Zhe, *On a New Theory of Human Rights*, p. 65.

16. Fu Xuezhe, *A Few Questions on Human Rights*, in Ye LiXuan and Li Sizhen (eds.) *On Human Rights*, Fujian: Fujian People's Publishing Company, 1991, pp. 318–19.

17. Lassa F. L. Oppenheim, in Hersch Lauterpacht (ed.) *International Law, A Treatise*, London: Longmans, Green and Co., 8th edn., 1955 Chapter IV, p. 371.

18. *The Essays of Einstein*, Part III, p. 82.
19. Karl Marx, 'On the Jewish Question', in Robert C. Tucker (ed.), *The Marx-Engels Reader*, New York: W.W. Norton & Co., 1972, p. 39.
20. See, *A Survey of the World's Human Rights Covenants*, Sichuan: Sichuan People's Press (Sichuan Renmin Chibanshe), 1990, pp. 759, 765.
21. *The Selected Works of Mao Zedong*, 2nd edn., Huiyang: Zhong Gong Huiyang Ti Wei Xuan Quan Pu, 1991, Part II, p. 768.
22. *Ibid*, Part III, p. 1070.
23. The Common Guidelines of the Chinese People's Political Consultative Conference, Article 5, *A Survey of the World's Human Rights Covenants*, 1991, p. 811.
24. Xiao Weiyun, *The Birth of Our Country's Present Constitution*, Beijing: Peking University Press (Beijing Daxue Chubanshe), 1986, p. 47.
25. See, Declaration of the Rights of Man, Article 11, in *A Survey of the World's Human Rights Covenants*, 1990, p. 296.
26. Lin Jia, *A Hundred Questions and Answers on Human Rights*, p. 215.

Human Rights and the Political Development of Contemporary China, 1979–1994

Zhu Feng

Since 4 June 1989, human rights in China have become an issue of increasing world concern. One of the main questions is how the present political development in China promotes and improves human rights. In fact, human rights have become the basic standard for measuring and judging trends in contemporary Chinese politics. Interactions between Hong Kong, Taiwan, and mainland China have also largely revolved around human rights in China.

Furthermore, human rights have become the hot issue in Chinese foreign relations. This has included United States discussions about whether to extend Most Favoured Nation (MFN) trading status to China based on its human rights record, European countries' attitude towards human rights in China in formulating bilateral relations, and reports concerning human rights in China by non-governmental organizations (NGOs) such as Amnesty International and Human Rights Watch. Undoubtedly, all agree that improving human rights should be a basic component of China's political development.

The post-Second World War period has produced a wide range of opinions concerning human rights. There are especially large differences of opinion between developed and developing, capitalist and socialist countries. This has become a subject of endless debate in the United Nations (UN) Human Rights Committee in Geneva. This debate has particularly focused on the relationship between sovereignty and human rights, that is on whether jurisdiction of human rights resides within a state or is subject to so-called 'universal' standards under international law. The Bangkok Declaration issued in April 1993 reflects some of these differences. As noted in Christine Loh's essay, the results of the United Nations World Conference on Human Rights held in Vienna in June of 1993 seemed to widen these differences, not narrow them.

Concerning the question of how to prioritize competing political, economic, and moral principles in promoting the improvement of human rights in China, there is still no final resolution within the international community. Many Western democratic countries appear to be following a so-called 'moral principle' of diplomacy. This principle, especially promoted by former US president Jimmy Carter, declares it the responsibility of a democratic country to promote international human rights protection, liberty, and democracy.

Despite the Carter policy, the US has often adopted double standards regarding human rights issues. Following what I call a 'political principle', a given country's strategic relationship with the US has often seemed more important than its human rights record in formulating US foreign policy. The US had for years generally ignored human rights abuses by capitalist regimes in Latin America and Asia, while condemning similar behaviour in socialists countries. The Carter administration had sought to reduce this neglect but did not completely abandon the policy. After what was generally considered a failed Carter policy the double standard was resumed. This trend has made it easy for countries on the receiving end of US criticism to reject the US policy as a sham.

After the cold war, the democratization and liberalization movements developed rapidly in former Eastern block and developing countries. Moreover, the military confrontation between East and West disappeared with the end of the cold war, causing many people in Western countries optimistically to believe that international discussion of human rights would transcend strategic political factors. Human rights seemed set to receive better protection in the international order. However, human rights are still being used as a weapon of intimidation from the free world against the few remaining socialist countries, such as China. It appears to be the hope of such countries that China will also abandon the socialist path. This hope has inspired trade sanctions against China, such as, for example the previous US MFN trade policies, where the US sought to pressure China to embrace more rapid political reform.

Nevertheless, the continuous high economic growth in China since 1990 shows the world that China is a potential highly profitable market. This has attracted many foreign businessmen to seek new commercial opportunities. As a result, international policy concerning the issue of human rights in China has shifted to a new 'economic principle'. Under this economic principle, to avoid a strong restrictive action by China, foreign governments should avoid disturbing China 'senselessly' about the question of human rights. For example, the French sale of jet fighters to Taiwan resulted in the cancellation of commercial contracts with French corporations. Under the economic principle this is to be avoided. The US administration's abandonment of the link between allowance of MFN status and human rights reflects similar concerns.

Therefore, the attitude and actions of the international community towards China's human rights problems are still unclear. The priority given moral, political, and economic principles has been changing, wrongly emphasized, and contradictory in Western policy towards China's human rights record. The principle of practical interest, a combination of political and economic considerations, is the dominant factor in determining Western policy towards human rights in China.

The expectation to improve China's human rights through international pressure shows a lack of common understanding of Chinese politics. The international community should see clearly that only criticizing China's human rights situation cannot bring about its improvement. The remainder of this essay will focus on the relationship between human rights and China's political reality. A more in-depth analysis of contemporary Chinese politics reveals the presence of positive human rights factors in China's political development.

The Relationship between Human Rights and Political Development

Human rights cannot be separated from contemporary political development. In modern times the term 'political development' refers to a process of political change which includes the renewal of political structures, the remoulding of the functions of the political system, and the formation of a system of popular participation. Although political scientists have many perspectives, most see the establishment of a democratic system and its effective running within a nation-state as the ultimate aim of political development. Under this general rubric, the emphasis may vary: some emphasize the development of administrative and legal systems; others emphasize popular mobilization and participation; others focus on stable and orderly change; and still others focus on solving the problems of authority and power. The mature democratic political model of contemporary industrial society can be the reference standard of contemporary political development.

Human rights are not only a strategy of political development but also its aim both in theory and in practice. Therefore human rights are inseparable from healthy political development. Any political development created by politics, economics, or culture which violates human rights is anti-democratic and will not be successful.

The evolving human rights concept has increasingly moved beyond the classical natural rights theory which simply emphasized civil and political rights. This concept has experienced a rich and practical development in the world's complex interactive processes. The Universal Declaration and the two international human rights covenants of the UN specify the generally accepted content of human rights to include both political and civil rights and economic, social, and cultural rights. This concept of human rights requires governments to see human rights not only as protecting of a citizen's safety and interest, but also as regulating the relationships between the State and society, the State and individuals, and between individuals.

Only when the political and civil rights of citizens are fully protected and universally enjoyed can a large and orderly mass mobilization with full participation be achieved. Under these conditions political life can reveal the interests of the masses and political management can be accomplished consistent with public opinion. Similarly, under the principles of economic, social, and cultural rights, modern society can practise equal and fair development and achieve orderly control of interpersonal relationships in the market economy.

The citizens' enjoyment of human rights provides the basis for the realization of the aims of political development, including social stability, continuous economic growth, and the increase of social welfare.[1] The experience of the developed industrial countries is revealed by their efforts, either actively or passively, to incorporate human rights into the development process. The key problem of developing countries is how, actively and voluntarily, to introduce the value of human rights into their political development.

In this aspect, recognition is the first step. Nowadays even the most totalitarian countries do not dare to ignore human rights totally and at least respect human rights in word if not in deed. However, it is still difficult self-consciously to inject the value of human rights into every aspect of political development. Although cultural relativism or traditional political ideology can be used as an excuse for the lack of recognition of human rights, as is done in the Bangkok Declaration, these arguments do not constitute a reasonable starting point for those who aspire to democratic political development. At the same time, no one can seriously argue that the specific content of human rights will be totally free of the influences of historical and cultural conditions, concerns about economic development and political reality.

On the basis of recognizing the value of human rights, political development in developing countries should consciously aim at separating politics and economics, state life and civil life, public affairs and personal affairs. This kind of separation is not simply a matter of dividing up tasks. The social composition of modern nation-states reflects different levels and forms of separation between economics and politics, the state and the individual. In a system of nearly total government and party control, such as existed previously in China, moving toward the separation mentioned here is a very complicated and painful process of partition and disconnection.

The meanings of separation are mainly the following: (1) the withdrawal of state political power. State political domination emerged by covering or controlling the entire scope of social life; the state must withdraw and return to its sphere of political and public affairs; and (2) during the process of withdrawal of political power, private affairs, that is the citizen and society, must be allowed to develop independently outside politics; the economic sphere must be allowed to develop independently according to the interests of citizens and society. Since the Second World War, the most common obstacle to achieving political democratization in developing countries, including China, has been the lack of independent and effective social power.[2]

China's political history of the 1950s, 1960s, and 1970s was one of expanding totalitarian control that aimed largely at eliminating independent and effective social power. The Anti-rightist Movement in the 1950s and the Four Clearance Movement in the early 1960s were both political suppressions under the rubric of purifying revolutionary spirit and puncturing anti-revolutionary power. When the Gang of Four was forced to relinquish power in 1976, Premier Hua Guofeng adopted the absolutely authoritative 'two whatevers' slogan in order to preserve the existing political composition under his own leadership and repress any development of social beliefs beyond political control.[3] This kind of political control is based on a personality cult.

As a practical matter, no matter whether a society is developing from totalitarianism or authoritarianism, the basic condition of democratic development is to break down the monopoly of politics over social and personal affairs, and thereby create an independent civil society.[4] The independent and free development of civil society produces the basic ability to be innovative in politics and to accomplish pluralizations of social and power structures.

In 1843, after the industrial revolution and the beginning of modernization in Western countries, Karl Marx discussed the relationship between politics and civil society. He felt that the breakdown of feudal societies had created independent individuals, who were citizens. At the same time, politics became a 'universality above the particular elements'; citizens divided from politics spawned the development of liberalism.[5] States declared human rights so as to protect the independent advancement of civil society and individuals from political intervention, and thereby to maintain individual freedom. According to Marx it was 'the most thorough emancipation of human society up to that time' and he called it 'political emancipation'.[6]

Professor Tang Tsou, in his splendid analysis of Chinese politics, argued that the step of 're-establishing civil society', was fundamental to the practical political development of China.[7] In the view of Professor Tsou, re-establishment of civil society is the crucial step for authoritarian countries to solve the problems of political underdevelopment and the lack of democracy. The key problem, then, is how to put the principles of separation of politics and economics, state life and civil life, public affairs and private affairs into practice. Through separation, the State removes its power from social and private spheres and creates the conditions for grass-roots promotion of democratic political development. This separation at least produces the following positive effects. First, it further accelerates the release of the State's authoritarian control over society. Although the decentralization of power in the economic sphere in China has stimulated economic development, economic decentralization alone is not enough. Decentralization in other spheres is required at the same time and is necessary in order to succeed at economic reform. As a result of economic reform, concepts of freedom and human rights begin to creep into discussion among Chinese people. This in turn further strengthens the demand from the community for establishing democratic politics.

Second, it makes it necessary to improve the Chinese legal system. The common understanding of the rule of law or 'legalism' among Chinese people is only to work according to rules and regulations. That people are not even working according to regulations and that regulations are poorly drafted makes the present Chinese legal system unhealthy. Even in ancient times, the 'declining of principles and order' and the 'degeneration of governmental rule' were always seen as the worst social maladies. Improving the existing Chinese legal system is mentioned every day but not much is done. Though many laws are drafted, implementation is lacking and there is little confidence in the legal system.

Third, society may attempt to establish the principle of checks and balances within national institutions. Ending current anti-democratic political domination depends on the existence of substitute political power. The existence of that kind of power in China still requires further development; it must be cultivated within civil society.

Thomas H. Marshall brilliantly analysed the effect of the evolution of civil society and human rights on the progress of Western societies. Although his research targeted developed countries, his theory is definitely meaningful to developing countries. He pointed out that respect for and practice of human rights requires 'a social framework that includes representative government, a mixed economy and a welfare state'.[8] This is exactly what we should look for in the recent developments of Chinese politics.

The Reality of China's Political Development since 1979

The political development of China since 1979 has been very dramatic. But just as the whole world was becoming hopeful about the reform and opening of China, the shots of 4 June 1989 turned the tide. Although the world's outrage has begun to subside, reports about the Chinese government locking up political offenders and repressing freedom of speech, etc., still cause heightened public concern. Nevertheless, in economic terms, China is enjoying a prosperity not heard of since before the 1840 Opium War. At the same time, Chinese politics are undergoing one of the most dramatic transformations in this century.

Modernization has continued apace in these last fifteen years. The Third Plenum of the Eleventh Central Committee of the Chinese Communist Party (CCP) in 1978 was the turning point in the relationship between the Chinese government and society. As noted above, the first three decades of Communist rule had been marked by expanding government control over society. Between the May 4th Movement in 1919 and 1949, there had been a tendency to devolve national power to society. Beginning in 1978 this tendency was renewed. Since then, in spite of occasional counter-tendencies, the state has generally tended to decentralize power and loosen its grip; the people are able to rest from the intense political pressures of the past and have started to rehabilitate society. This is the most significant positive factor in China's human rights picture. The next two sections will consider the process of political change before outlining, in the final part of this essay, the evolution of China's concept of human rights.

The Establishment of Political Control, 1949–1979

The Communist government, established after the success of the 1949 revolution, is the dual product of the trend of radical thought and social mobilization since the May 4th Movement. The revolution caused a grand change in Chinese society. The most explicit and profound change is that the power of the State and party penetrated into every corner of society. So-called political activities became the central content of all social activities.

John Lewis notes that this situation reached its high tide in the 1950s. In terms of economics, the joint state-private ownership system in the cities was fully established in 1956. At the same time, transition from the 'mutual aid production group' (volunteer co-operation and expense-sharing among village farmers who owned their land) to the 'advanced level production group' (State imposed co-operation among farmers in a larger area) was in progress in the countryside. In 1957, Mao Zedong actively advocated the establishment of people's communes (full public ownership and control) in the countryside. All the above subjected the economic life of Chinese society under socialism to official control.

In terms of ideology and consciousness, the Anti-rightist Movement, which started in 1956 as a grand clearance movement, exercised strong control over thinking and speech in every stratum of social life. In terms of administration, from the founding of the People's Republic of China (PRC) to 1957, an administrative system based on the different organizational levels of the party, and the Communist Youth League was widely established in every community and administrative unit in China. Party membership increased from two million in 1949 to sixteen million by the late 1950s whilst absolute belief in socialism and loyalty towards the party flourished.

Although the Great Leap Forward, advocated by Mao in 1958, was a naïve practice of idealism, it was the first exercise of power by the new Chinese system which clearly demonstrated the complete integration of politics and society under the one-party state. Lewis further observes that the principle contained in the statement 'the party is the state, the state is society and the society is the individual' actually became manifest.[9] The near worship of individual political leaders, dictatorship, and intensification of power were overflowing everywhere. This happened not only with respect to Mao, but also with respect to regional officials and cadres of the party. The revolutionary integration of party and state created the condition for Mao to launch the Cultural Revolution, and reached its zenith during the Cultural Revolution. Professor Tang Tsou uses the concept 'totalism', a term which he prefers to the term 'totalitarianism', to explain the evident characteristics of the above trends in Chinese politics after 1949. He indicates that the basic characteristic of totalism was that the society lacked any area upon which institutions of political power could not infringe.[10] In other words, individual or collective freedom and rights were totally decided by the authorized political institutions; and the power of these authorized political institutions was not restricted. Moreover, the political culture of 'party is state' dictatorship completely concealed the human soul and created an anti-intellectualism; consequently, politics replaced the protection usually offered by morality, public opinion, and consciousness.

Leszek Kolakowski has described vividly the characteristics of totalitarian systems in socialist countries, and analysed the negative effect of the party-state on freedom and rights:

> I take the word totalitarian in a commonly used sense, meaning a political system where all social ties have been entirely replaced by state-imposed organizations and where, consequently, all groups and all individuals are supposed to act only for goals which are both the goals of the state and are defined as such by the state. In other words, an ideal totalitarian system would consist of utter destruction of civil society, wherein the state and its organizational instruments are the only forms of social life, where all kinds of human activities — economic, intellectual, political, cultural — are allowed and ordered (the distinction between what is allowed and what is ordered tending to disappear) only to the extent of being at the service of state goals (again, as defined by the state). Every individual (including the rulers themselves) is considered the property of the state.[11]

No matter what kind of theoretical concept we use to analyse the neglect of human rights during the Mao Zedong period, we are still left with an empirical truism: the State's (or entities that look like states) complete intervention and control over social life precludes the protection of human rights. Under this reality, human beings are only an inferior tool for the utopian revolution. Even Mao once praised the instrumental value and role of people, saying, 'As long as there are people, every kind of miracle can be performed.'[12]

But in Mao's mind, he only had the idea of sacrificing one-self for the revolution. He did not have the idea that the freedom and rights of individuals should be fulfilled or that this be treated as the starting point of politics. Besides, Mao always looked favourably on the earlier revolutionary era — especially the self-denial and idealism of the revolution aroused by the hardest conditions during Yenan period in the 1930s.

Mao's distain of materialism and emphasis on idealism manifested itself in two ways: Mao was against individual society members actively raising demands relating to their own material interest; he thought this was selfish and that it would bring about anarchism. On the other hand, under a state-led economy, Mao was against using material incentives to induce production. This kind of ascetic political theory precludes using economic means to develop the economy; economic departments rather depended on the use of empty dogma such as 'put politics in command' and 'grasp revolution, promote production' (*zhua ge ming, cu sheng chan*) as the means to encourage economic growth. The discrepancy between the poverty resulting from this kind of socialism, and Mao's revolutionary ideal was evident.

Mao raised the famous principle of 'class struggle' to insert an imaginary element of 'life and death' struggle into the remaining gap between politics and society. He aimed to overcome the remaining resistance to political control through the vehicle of mass movements. When this strategy was challenged, Mao used the notion of 'people's war' to develop a personality cult to enable him to block all challenges. This produced Mao's greatest failure. The Cultural Revolution was the most extreme form of the idea that the 'party is the state'. It not only brought up the darkest hour of human rights in modern Chinese history but also produced the total collapse of democracy, legalism, and the economy.

The Opening, 1979-Present

The Third Plenum of the Eleventh Central Committee of the Chinese Communist Party (CCP) in 1978 was the starting point of the reform and open policy of China. From 1979 the 'party is state' ideology has been in decline. The significance of the Third Plenum was to announce the death of Mao's 'endless revolution under the proletarian dictatorship', put aside Mao's political authority and political thinking, give people the right to adjust, and offer new explanations of Mao's thinking.[13] The process of separating political life and civil life in China began. At this juncture the contemporary grass-roots demand for human rights also began.

In studying the development of Chinese politics since 1979, the student strikes of the 1980s — which I will discuss below — have a special significance. Not only did they lead to the political demise of two general secretaries of the CCP, Hu Yaobang and Zhao Ziyang, but they also represented the culmination of political trends begun in the Democracy Wall Movement in the late 1970s. Although the Democracy Wall Movement was largely an intellectual, rather than a student, movement, it established a form of popular movement which would later be taken up by students. The idea of popular political participation in opposition to the government was established; the ideas of democracy and freedom became widely popular among students.

The free election of a deputy to the National People's Congress (NPC) from the Hai Dian District inside Beijing University during the fall of 1980 marked the formal beginning of contemporary Chinese campus upheaval.[14] In fact, a student strike at this time became a people's initiative movement seeking freedom, democracy, and human rights. Though the gist of the early student movement was to support the reform and opening up of the existing political regime, it became, in essence, a grand challenge concerning the lack of democracy and the rule of law.

From the beginning, Deng Xiaoping recognized the danger to existing authority created by student strikes. He stressed several times that 'democracy without the leading role of the Party, and democracy without discipline and order are definitely not socialist democracy.'[15] However, Deng may also have seen some advantages for his own policies in the student strikes: the support for reform evident in student upheaval demonstrated the popularity of his policies. This helped him to contend with the leftist opposition to his economic reforms. The March 1981 Beijing University student slogan 'unite and develop China' and the 1984 National Day banner proclaiming 'Xiaoping, how are you?' (*Xiaoping, nin hao?*) made Deng feel the students supported him. At the same time, permitting the students to strike demonstrated to the world his open and liberal image.

During the Mao Zedong era, mass rallies, assemblies, and demonstrations were quite normal, but these were in service of the existing authorities, not against them. The aim was to make use of the blind zeal of the people to support the existing policy. It seemed that Deng envisioned the student movement from the early 1980s in the same way, even though certain differences were apparent. By the 1980s students and intellectuals had acquired a greater understanding of the outside world and were attracted to its liberal and democratic values. Students, awakened to democracy were not inclined to submit their zeal to the existing authority.

None the less, in the mid-1980s, Deng adopted a pragmatic route. This allowed space for intellectuals to continue to express their opinions, as was evident in the academic salons from which such intellectuals as Liu Binyan produced essays. In late 1986, however, anger over price increases and political ineptitude caused student strikes and demonstrations in Beijing and Shanghai. While the Democracy Wall Movement had aimed mainly at the excesses of the Cultural Revolution, this was the first major challenge to the government after the implementation of reform. The student strikes in 1986 and 1987 reflected the popular view that the policy of initiating economic reform without political reform was impossible.

One of the consequences of this political unrest was the fall from power of the reformist CCP General Secretary Hu Yaobang. His sin was 'not doing his best to counter-attack bourgeois liberalism'. He was indeed a scapegoat. Deng aimed to demonstrate clearly that China could not practise 'bourgeois democracy'; 'stability and consolidation' were more important. On the one hand, he indicated his intention to persist in reform, saying, 'if there is any imperfection, it is because we have not opened enough'; on the other hand, he demanded 'a clear-cut stand against bourgeois liberalism' and insisted on the 'four basic principles'.[16] He apparently felt he had no choice but to persist in this contradiction. A grand act of repression would only cause his reputation and achievements to be destroyed. He told the Prime Minister of Japan who visited on 13 January 1987, 'We have to avoid the spread of student demonstrations; however, even it spreads ten times, this will not affect our route and our policy because the policies we are pursuing now are correct; our people get the benefits.'[17]

The political development from 1987 to 1989 mocked Deng's ideas. Since many problems created by institutional changes could not be quickly resolved, inflation became worse and the citizens' living standards declined. Bureaucratic degeneration worsened, the structural inequality of social distribution widened, and agricultural production decreased. Frustration and discontent among the people increased. As officials looked for ways to make more money, the principle that 'socialist officials are the servants of the people' was violated. That some officials were lining their own pockets while holding high the banner of socialism produced public anger. At the same time, the growing number of independent entrepreneurs put their weight behind reform. These forces converged to produce the 1989 Democracy Movement.

In 1987 Deng's stand against student demonstrations hardened. However, by this stage he was heavily burdened by struggles within the party over the course of reform and had little time to confront an outside challenge. As a result, he compromised and again showed his tolerance toward students, saying that 'a few students going to the streets could not affect the overall situation'. He believed the best course was to intensify party guidance for young students, explain where the problems were, and specifically rectify intellectuals. A few intellectuals who opposed the party, such as physicist Fang Lizhi, Wang Luosui, and journalist Liu Binyan, were expelled from the party.

The weakening of political control in the 1980s began the separation process of politics and society. Once the old authoritative system was challenged, however, the government could show no consideration and endeavoured to resist the separating process and resume authoritative control of politics over society. Though the development of the CCP was weakened in 1989, political authority did not weaken much. The CCP still held absolute control over the military and the police. In China, Deng and his colleagues had acquired power and authority by experiencing the long revolution. Under the totalitarian system of the CCP power and authority were consolidated. This is the reason why Deng was more fortunate than his Eastern European counterparts in his ability to gain the support of military leaders for reform.

Deng had already warned of the need to be willing to use strong measures as early as 1986. For Deng, with the revolt represented by the student strikes coming from within society he had to be prepared to take all measures necessary to preserve his power. The flag of human rights lifted by the student and intellectual movements weakened the authority of the party-state but did not weaken its power. The June 4th Movement did not raise any broad demand for human rights. It only demanded an equal dialogue with government, freedom of speech and assembly, and basic participation in politics. These are all very common civil and political rights and are stipulated in the 1982 Chinese Constitution. The student movement was repressed as a revolt.

The separation process of politics and society is a restructuring, dividing, and mobilizing process. Only when this process lasts and continuously develops can a pluralist social reality and political base for democracy and human rights be produced. The process includes the rise of a middle class, widening of interest groups, the acceptance of the new rules of the game for politics, and the deepening of the new political theory in the people's minds. The most important thing is a change in the economic system to reduce the government's hold on economic power.

The failure of the June 4th demonstration is easy to understand if one considers the underdeveloped political and social separating process of China at that time. When the dissidents of the June 4th Movement analyze the reasons for the failure of that movement they frankly admit that 'there was great contrast between the immense zeal of the masses and the underdeveloped theory of the intellectuals'; they lacked a mature attitude to lead the June 4th Movement. Professor Tang Tsou also points out that the June 4th Movement could not produce a kind of institutional structure and social psychological expectation for the Chinese people involved to resolve problems rationally.[18] This left them to solve problems by using negotiation, bargaining, and a set of endless compromises and mutual adjustments.

The main hope for human rights in China does not come from overseas dissidents or pressure from the West. It can only come from the present political development of China. The tragic result on 4 June 1989 set back, but did not block permanently the process of separation of politics and society; nor did it conclude the reforming process. Deng himself repeatedly emphasized that reform and opening must continue firmly and unshakeably: 'Except that individual concepts need to be modified, the basic route and the essential orientation and policy will not be changed.'[19] Deng still talked like that after June 4th, indicating that he did not want to lock the door of reform; he recognized that, although it created a consciousness of self-determination and freedom in the Chinese people it was impossible to prevent such pounding at the door. Sensing the danger to the existing system, he said, 'This disturbance will come sooner or later. This is determined by the big international climate and China's own small climate.'[20]

If it is to be said that the Third Plenum of the Central Committee made the CCP cast off the ideological constraints of Mao; after June 4th, the CCP cast off Mao's political tactics. Because of Deng, a renewal of the CCP was initiated. The number of political offenders arrested, compared with the Mao era, was much lower. Concerning human rights, Chinese politics have indeed improved a lot, though there is still a long way to go. This is evident in comparing recent arrests with the twenty million people subjected to persecution during the anti-rightist period and the fifty-five million people tortured during the Cultural Revolution.

However, the misfortune in Deng's response to these developments was that he, on the one hand, continued to implement reforms but, on the other hand, intensified the actualization of the four basic principles. The latter requires intensifying control over ideology, speech, association, and assembly. As a result, after June 4th, China entered its most restrictive period since 1979 of suppressing thinking and speech. This included consolidating the Party, strengthening the cleansing of the minds of youth and students, elevating the status of ideological guidelines, increasing censorship of publishing and mass media, and taking measures (including numerous arrests) against those holding different political viewpoints. Deng and the leadership also fostered a strong and uncompromising nationalism to block human rights pressure from the West. This sentiment has been encouraged in the population and has been used as a weapon to deflect outside criticism of China's human rights record.

Many scholars believe that improvement in human rights in China should rely on economic development. This is definitely correct. However, with the economic growth, especially during the period between 1990 and 1994, averaging more than 12 per cent annually, why is the opposition between the state and society still widening but not narrowing? It seems that setting aside a few Marxist economic doctrines is not enough. The government must extend the freedom and human rights of people; people also need a sense of full democratic participation.

In the spring of 1992, Deng moved the clock forward for the development of China again, and delivered his famous speech, made during his visit to the South, about the importance of economic liberalization. The speech did not contain any new ideas but, instead, criticized the extreme leftist argument that 'the major danger of peaceful evolution comes from the economic sphere', and pointed out that 'China has to beware of being rightist, but mainly to avoid being leftist'.[21]

Since 1992, there have been radical changes in economic life, though problems remain. Media coverage of this period has witnessed improved economic reporting and increased probing of the social and political consequences of growth. The growth of the economy has at last pushed China to make some visible changes and improvements in human rights. First, China has started to treat human rights as an important aim of public policy. While this has not reached significantly into the area of political rights, it has affected law reform resulting in better laws to protect women and children, as well as property. Recent annual reports to the NPC have even included the topic of human rights. In June 1994 the government also started providing basic social welfare for those who have fallen through the net of the economic system.

Second, provision of legal restraints on public officials have increased. China has always been a 'official-oriented' country. Officials have traditionally had a casual attitude toward the common people. The administrative regulations against official abuse are increasing, and the power of public opinion is growing stronger. Third, the procedural laws to protect human rights are also expanding. How to provide a fair and correct legal process is fundamental to the protection of human rights. The present Chinese legal system is very weak and the quality of the responsible officials is commonly quite bad. Political interference in the application of laws has always been a serious problem. The following section examines the underlying political attitude toward human rights often reflected in the application of law.

Chinese Political Understanding of Human Rights

After the triumph of the 1949 revolution, the Chinese Communist Party, when its power was consolidated, developed the one-party system. Human rights were sacrificed to the consolidation of power. The Land Reform Program of 1950 to 1953, though successfully solving the land problems of peasants, caused severe damage to human rights in that land owners were treated very badly and their rights were often ignored. The so-called 'Common Program' (a preliminary constitutional document) of 1949 stipulated the basic rights enjoyed by Chinese citizens. The 1954 Constitution, Chapter 3, also provided an extensive catalogue of basic rights. These rights guarantees were severely diminished in the two constitutions promulgated in 1975 and 1978 during the Cultural Revolution. The 1975 Constitution cancelled the article which stated that the state would provide protection for the rights and freedom of citizens. This Constitution also, ridiculously, included 'upholding the leadership of the CCP and the socialist system' as a basic right and obligation of Chinese citizens. During the Cultural Revolution the basic freedoms of citizens did not have any protection from arbitrary political control.

There were many reasons for this situation. First, Marxism, according to the CCP, was required to emphasize class struggle, cancel private ownership, and implement, even resorting to violence if necessary, proletarian dictatorship. Second, Mao considered himself a genuine Marxist and sought to implement its classical requirements in Chinese socialism; the CCP must clearly break with the 'bourgeoisie'. Third, the political ideology and political strategy of Mao were deeply affected by traditional Chinese authoritarianism. His understanding and application of power were completely unrestricted by human rights. Fourth, the long struggle of the CCP had made Mao himself sense the seriousness of any opposition. As a result, Mao embraced a simple dichotomy — if a man is not an enemy, he is a friend; if he is not a friend, he is an enemy. Human rights aim to deal with enemies without reference to principle and with class compromise. This is what Mao criticized the most.

Mao's understanding of human rights can be summarized in three points. First, human rights belonged to the bourgeoisie, and could not be applied to the proletariat; second, due to the needs of revolution and class struggle, human rights should not be taken seriously because 'human' is only a concept without reference to class differences (Mao only embraced the idea of class rights, but not the idea of human rights) Third, even if 'the people of the nation' belonged to the right class, they held rights only collectively, not as individuals. In short, according to Mao and the party leadership, China did not need human rights.

The Third Plenum of the Eleventh Central Committee of the CCP in 1978 marked a grand adjustment for the CCP in both ideology and policy. However, this adjustment was not complete and comprehensive. Deng did review many mishandled cases and abandoned the absolute authority that Mao had exercised. However, his exposition and criticism of Mao's theory concentrated only on doing away with such anachronisms as continuous revolution, intense class struggle, and individual worship, but did not touch seriously upon the profound ideological, theoretical, and systematic reasons for Mao's mistakes.

The adjustment of the Third Plenum of the Eleventh Central Committee of the CCP is not only the result of the introspection and struggle over the Party's ideology, but also the consequence of an internal power struggle. In fact, the theoretical preparation for the power struggle had started in the spring of 1978. The editorial entitled 'Practice is the Only Standard for Testifying the Truth,' whose title was prominently displayed on the cover of the intellectual newspaper *Guang Ming Ri Bao* on 11 May 1978, sounded the call to criticize and denounce Mao and his fellow ideologues.

When the CCP opened the Twelfth National People's Congress in September 1982, Deng's unshakeable position in Chinese politics was secured. His slogan at this meeting was 'Combine the common truth of Marxism with the concrete reality of our country; walk our own road, establish socialism with Chinese characteristics.' Subsequently, both the Thirteenth Party Central Committee meetings in 1989 and the Fourteenth

Party Central Committee meetings in 1992 were only to adjust and develop further Deng's ideology.

'Socialism with Chinese characteristics' is neither a well-organized theory nor a predetermined practice. It merely advances the basic principles that: (1) China must insist on advancing under socialism and the leadership of the CCP; (2) the economy is always the highest priority; and (3) the paths of stability and consolidation must focus on the present, not the future. These principles are almost contradictory. They do not have a tight and well-organized logic. Under this rubric there is a tendency to shift back and forth from anti-leftist to anti-rightist policies, as dictated by the exigencies of the moment. This, nevertheless, represents a major shift from Mao's theories. Revolutionary mass movements are abandoned, along with political asceticism and the command of politics over economics.

Although the Democracy Wall Movement between 1978 and 1979 was brief, its numerous street posters revealed a yearning for democracy, liberty, legalism, and human rights. People had already started to advocate new political ideas. 'The Nineteen Articles of Human Rights', published at that time, was a representative publication.[22] A society that had grown used to Maoist clothes was even urged to 'dress freely'. The 'fifth modernization', political democratization, was widely advocated.

In spite of these calls for democracy, Deng still in some respects followed the theoretical perspective of Mao, insisting on class-based analysis: 'Democracy for Chinese people nowadays can only be the socialist democracy with the people as the masters; it cannot be the individualistic democracy of the bourgeoisie. People's democracy is inseparable from dictatorship against the people's enemies.'[23] Wei Jingshen and Wang Xizhe, the two most prominent dissidents of the Democracy Wall Movement, advocated 'bourgeois human rights', so they became the targets of the dictatorship; they became the 'enemy'; they were jailed.

According to this view, individual freedom and rights are conditional. This condition is not the law mentioned by Kant or Locke, it is rather the needs of the party-state. 'Under the socialist system, individual interest should give way to collective interest; interests of the parts should give way to the interest of the whole; temporary interest should give way to long-term interest.'[24] Why is this so? The reason, according to Deng, is that under the socialist system all of the above interests are integrated.[25] This ignores the increased expectations of the people as the economy develops.

Professor Samuel P. Huntington has pointed out, 'Economic development itself is a continuous unstable process, which is a new policy for the fulfilment of the people's demands. However, it usually further enlarges their wants.'[26] Chinese intellectuals took the role of the first mobilized people during the changing and unstable social conditions of the mid-1980s. On the one hand, they devoted themselves to the introduction of Western technology and management experience. On the other hand, they also started to introduce democracy and liberal theory from the West. It became a great challenge to the CCP political system.

If one reflects on the developments in this period, it is easy to see that the theoretical foundation for these difficulties was laid much earlier in the failure of the CCP to come to grips with the implications of its reform policy. In the post-1979 period, in its first article on human rights entitled 'How Marxism Looks at the Issue of Human Rights,' the CCP denied that there existed a problem of human rights in China: 'Our socialist country is the first country which has solved the problem of the people's right to democracy in human history. Only socialist countries have the broadest basis for the right to democracy. Such a right is incompatible with capitalism. . . . Human rights is only a slogan of the bourgeoisie.'[27] This article, however, attributed the failure of democracy and human rights in China to the mistakes of Lin Biao and the Gang of Four during the Cultural Revolution. Its conclusion was only to follow the four basic principles.

In April 1979, the *Shanghai Wen Hui Bao* published an article entitled 'Human Rights is the Slogan of the Bourgeoisie'.[28] This article argued once again that the socialist system already protected the rights of the people. People who demanded human rights were labeled 'reactionary elements' who 'had ulterior motives hostile to socialism' and 'lacked an accurate conception of human rights'. This article accurately recognized that human rights would only weaken proletarian dictatorship and intensify opposition to authority. The attitudes towards human rights reflected in this article appear to be the product of a theoretical deep-freeze among elder leaders.

Nevertheless, Deng has indeed tried to prevent the CCP from repeating the failures of the past thirty years. As the backbone of the CCP's renovation, his wealth of political experience and pragmatism have allowed him to switch the engines of reform on and off. Within the confines of certain theoretical commitments he has been responsive to public concerns in the reform process.

The Fifth Meeting of the Fifth National People's Congress in November 1982 passed the 1982 Constitution. Chapter 2, entitled the 'Fundamental Rights and Duties of Citizens', increased the rights guarantees to twenty-four articles. This restored the Western constitutional style and many of the rights of the 1954 Constitution. Such rights as freedom of speech, equality, the right to vote, etc., were listed, at least as aspirational rights. Only the preamble makes reference to the role of the 'Party' or 'socialism'. Though there were further amendments in 1988 and 1993, these amendments did not affect these basic guarantees.

The Chinese authorities believe law is the reflection of the ruling class's ideology, the tool for class domination. Therefore, the socialist constitution should also reflect proletarian dictatorship and national socialism. Nevertheless, the Constitution's chapter on the rights and duties of citizens now deviates slightly from this principle. It no longer categorizes people as either friends or enemies. It adopts the neutral term 'citizen' as the legal term to refer to the Chinese people. It also legally separates human rights from the four basic principles. Unfortunately, there is no effective system to implement the human rights guarantees. You may say China has a constitution but not constitutionalism.[29]

Essentially these constitutional difficulties stem from the CCP leadership's refusal to relinquish control. Deng has always wanted to retain control of reform in his own hands — keeping for himself the image of a 'general planner'.

However, to a certain extent, Deng himself is a major advocate of liberalization in China. His economic reform is just the opposite of Marxism and Maoism. This in-depth economic reform has caused many Chinese intellectuals to challenge the contradiction between an open economy and tightly controlled ideology. Popular attitudes are changing, even within the party. Su Zhaozhi, a well-known dissenter, was the director of the now defunct official Institute of

Marxism and Socialism; Hu Yaobang and Zhao Ziyang, the two former general secretaries of the CCP, both interpreted 'democracy' and 'liberty' differently than Deng. Many chief editors of newspapers and journals are reluctant to go along with Deng's criticisms of 'liberalization'.

Deng's attitude toward human rights triumphed when the CCP dealt with the Tiananmen student movement in 1989. The editorial entitled 'Hoisting a Clear Flag to Fight Against the Riots' on the cover of the 26 April 1989 *People's Daily* (*Renmin Rebao*) defined the student strike as a riot instigated by a minority. This profoundly enraged many Chinese people. Afterwards, the unequal power confrontation between the Party seniors and the students resulted in the June 4th tragedy.

There appears to be growing recognition that it is difficult to forget the tragic events of 4 June 1989 and that a new response to human rights demands is required. A white paper entitled 'Human Rights in China', published in 1991 (in five languages), signalled a new policy to confront the human rights debate head-on.[30] It also reflected an adjustment in the CCP's basic theoretical position. It admits that the achievement of human rights is an important objective that oversteps any class boundaries: 'Enjoying full human rights is the ideal that has long been sought by mankind.'

With the rapid development of the Chinese economy since 1992, China's engagement in the international economy has steadily increased its involvement in world affairs. The Chinese Foreign Minister Qian Qichen indicated in April 1994 that China supports the international human rights bills, including the Universal Declaration of Human Rights.[31] This means that China has begun to accept international human rights standards. Such acceptance would be an adjustment even from China's stand on the Bangkok Declaration in April 1993, wherein China argued it was impossible to accept a common human rights standard.

Conclusion

Modernization of Chinese politics is impossible to accomplish without protection of human rights. Protection of human rights in turn depends on political reforms which aid the process of weaving human rights ideas into the social fabric.

This is a step by step process which requires movement on both fronts simultaneously. Respect for and protection of human rights not only requires an appropriate legal process, but also requires a value basis for the establishment of democratic ideology. Only on this basis can a truly fair, liberal, and civilized modern political system be built.

For developing countries, developing human rights need not mean adopting fully the specific contents of human rights employed in the West, though some of its core values seem essential. In application the specific contents of rights are always affected by the economic development level, historical traditions, cultural background, and political reality of the society involved. For Western countries to demand that developing countries have the same human rights conditions is unreasonable.

The development of human rights is a step by step process. The developmental experience of the West illustrates the fact that human rights first existed as an idea or attitude in the West and was later established by politics and law as a core value. When a human rights-oriented system came into existence there finally came the enrichment and perfection of the contents of human rights.

This kind of development depends on democracy at all levels of society. Democracy is the product of full political development. By the same token, the full development of democracy depends on human rights. What China needs at present is greater freedom and the rule of law. These have a direct relationship to human rights and will advance the popularity of human rights thinking. This will in turn aid the processes of democratic development. In this context, statistics indicate that the existing Chinese social order is facing bigger challenges. There are four million children deprived of education and nearly eight million unemployed or underemployed workers; worker-safety and other conditions are also of grave concern.[32] In some respects, the human rights conditions in China seem to be worse than in 1979.

Nevertheless, the political developments that have occurred in China since 1979 have had significant implications for the promotion of human rights and democratic development there. The reform and opening since 1979 has caused the breakdown of politics' overwhelming grip over society. State and society are separating. Under these conditions the popularity of human rights values among Chinese people is growing stronger day by day.

Notes

1. Jeremy Waldron, *Liberal Rights: Collected Papers 1981–1991*, Cambridge: Cambridge University Press, 1991, p. 55.
2. Martin K. Whyte, 'Urban China: A Civil Society in the Making' in Arthur L. Rosenbaum (ed.), *State and Society in China*, Boulder: Westview Press, Inc., 1992, p. 29.
3. The 'two-whatevers' slogan was: 'We will resolutely uphold whatever policy decisions Chairman Mao made, and unswervingly follow whatever instruction Mao gave,' and was adopted by Hua in trying to assume the mantle of Mao.
4. Adam Seligman (ed.), *The Idea of Civil Society*, New York: The Free Press, 1992, p. 168.
5. Karl Marx, 'On the Jewish Question', in Robert C. Tucker (ed.), *The Marx-Engels Reader*, New York: W. W. Norton & Company, Inc., 1972, p. 31.
6. *Ibid*, pp. 29–30.
7. Tang Tsou, *The Politics of China in the Twentieth Century*, Hong Kong: Oxford University Press, 1994, p. 202.
8. Thomas H. Marshall and Tom Bottomore, *Citizenship and Social Class*, London: Pluto Press, 1992, p. 25.
9. John W. Lewis, *Leadership in Communist China*, Ithaca, New York: Cornell University, 1963, pp. 108–120.
10. Tang Tsou, *The Politics of China in Twentieth Century*, p. 3. According to Professor Tsou's definition, totalism is more substantial than totalitarianism due to the penetration of political power into other spheres of social life.
11. Leszek Kolakowski, 'Marxist Roots of Stalinism', cited in Simon Leys, 'Human Rights in China', *National Review*, No. 12, 1978, p. 7.
12. *The Selected Papers of Mao Zedong*, Vol. 4, Beijing: People's Press, 1991, p. 1512.
13. Tang Tsou, *The Cultural Revolution and Post-Mao Reform: A Historical Perspective*, Chicago: The University of Chicago Press, 1986, p. 219.
14. It was an experimental free election campaign on campus for the District People's Congress in Beijing. Although this type of open election was later forbidden, candidates of Beijing University at that time like Hu Ping and Wang Juntao have since become well-known dissidents.
15. *Select Papers of Deng Xiaoping*, Vol. 1 (in Chinese), Beijing: People Press, 1983, p. 157.

16. *Selected Papers of Den Xiaping,* Vol. 3, p. 194. The so-called 'four basic principles' include upholding the socialist road, leadership of the Communist Party, dictatorship of the proletariat, and Marxism, Leninism, and Mao Zedong thought.
17. *Ibid,* p. 200.
18. Leys, 'Human Rights in China', p. 136.
19. *Selected Papers of Deng Xiaoping,* Vol. 3, p. 305.
20. *Ibid.*
21. *Selected Papers of Deng Xiaoping,* p. 375.
22. 'The Nineteen Articles of Human Rights,' *Chinese Human Rights* (Zhongguo Ren Quan) (Taipei: Chinese Communist Party Studies Press (Zhong Gong Yan Jiu Za Zhi She), 1980), p. 187.
23. *Selected Papers of Deng Xiaoping,* Vol. 1, p. 163.
24. *Ibid,* Vol. 1, p. 164.
25. *Ibid.*
26. Samuel P. Huntington, *Political Order in a Changing Society,* New Haven: Yale University Press, 1968, p. 247.
27. 'How Marxism Looks at the Issue of Human Rights,' (in Chinese) *Red Flag Magazine,* (Hong Qi Za Zhi), Vol. 6, 1979.
28. 'Human Rights is the Slogan of the Bourgeoisie', (in Chinese) *Shanghai Wen Hui Bao,* 8 April 1979.
29. Michael C. Davis, *Constitutional Confrontation in Hong Kong,* London: Macmillan Press, 1989.
30. *Human Rights in China,* Beijing: Information Office of the State Council, 1991.
31. *People's Daily* (Renmin Rebao), 15 April 1994.
32. *China Daily,* 2 April 1994, p. 4.

Part V
The Human Rights Process

The Vienna Process and the Importance of Universal Standards in Asia

Christine Loh

Any consideration of the application of human rights in China or Asia must give due regard to the evolving international standards and practices in this regard. The international practices offer the context in which domestic human rights practices take place. There are many international organizations and activities engaging the human rights debate. To the extent that these activities reflect strong commitment they may represent standards to which governments must adhere. The United Nations (UN) often provides the venue for this human rights discourse and is a good starting point from which to consider the international practices and their application to Asia.

Though it is the most well established institutionalized forum for discussing human rights, the United Nations is oftened hampered by a lack of resources and will when it comes to practical and effective action regarding human rights. Despite various declarations, covenants, resolutions, and guidelines, politics have often cut across the functions of promoting and protecting human rights. Recent events in Somalia, Bosnia-Herzegovina, and Rwanda demonstrate the UN's limitations when confronted with situations demanding urgent and concrete responses.

However, the UN does have the capacity to provoke and focus world attention. The recent Vienna process reinvigorated the debate on human rights. Originally conceived as an occasion for reaffirming universal human rights standards in the post-cold war era, the Vienna process became instead a battleground for East-West and North-South ideologies and politics. Asian governments took the lead in challenging the application of universal standards. The UN World Conference on Human Rights held from 14 June to 25 June 1993 in Vienna was the second such UN gathering. The first was held 25 years earlier at Teheran where the proclamation issued stated that, 'The primary aim of the United Nations in the sphere of human rights is the achievement of each individual of the maximum freedom and dignity' but acknowledged that 'the widening gap between the economically developed and the developing countries impedes the realization of human rights in the international community.'

Human rights issues lie at the heart of modern political discourse. They raise questions about the essential values of society, about the relationship between the state and the individual, between members of the international community, and between international and domestic law. As a context for considering Asian arguments about human rights, as well as Chinese practices, addressed throughout the present volume, this essay considers the existing international regime and practices culminating in the Vienna process. After introducing international instruments and practices in the following three sections, this essay addresses the Vienna process and its implications for the evolving conception of human rights. This analysis rejects the argument that Asia is somehow excluded from participation in this conception.

International Human Rights Instruments

Upon formation of the UN in 1945, the UN Charter affirmed 'faith in fundamental human rights, in the dignity and worth of the human person, in the equal rights of men and women and of nations large and small'. Members pledged to 'take joint and separate action in cooperation' with the UN to promote 'universal respect for, and observance of, human rights and fundamental freedoms for all without distinction as to race, sex, language or religion.' International lawyer, Hersch Lauterpacht, said of the Charter that 'the individual has acquired a status and a stature which have transformed him from an object of international compassion into a subject of international right.'[1]

The Universal Declaration of Human Rights, passed by the General Assembly on 10 December 1948, is an international bill of rights. Its Preamble starts with the assertion that 'the inherent dignity' of the individual, and not the state or its government, is the 'foundation of freedom, justice and peace in the world'. The Preamble continues, 'disregard and contempt for human rights have resulted in barbarous acts which have outraged the conscience of mankind.' It is essential, therefore, 'that human rights should be protected by law'. These assertions, if members states are to honour them, require them to introduce domestic legislation and to set up the necessary implementation machinery.

The Declaration, as John Humpries writes, is

> the work of literally thousands of people who contributed to the drafting process through United Nations bodies, the specialized agencies, and non-governmental agencies. Although Western influences were undoubtedly the strongest, both Marxist-Leninist theory and community practice were important, as were the claims of the politically and economically dependent countries.[2]

This reflection of history is not shared by Lee Kuan Yew, Senior Minister of Singapore. He described the origin of the Declaration as follows:

> It (the Declaration) was written up by the victorious powers at the end of World War II, which meant the US and the British primarily, as well as the French, the Russians and the Chinese. The Russians did not believe a single word of what they signed in the declaration. The Chinese were in such a mess they had to pretend they were espousing the inalienable rights and liberties of man to get American aid to fight the communists, who were threatening them in 1945. So the victors settled the Universal Declaration of Human Rights, and every nation that joined the UN was presumed to have subscribed to it.[3]

Charles Habib Malik, who chaired the committee which presented the final text to the UN General Assembly, recalled events somewhat differently. He said that:

> The Declaration was a composite product of all cultures and nations pooling in their wisdom and insight. The Atlantic world stressed principally civil, political, and personal liberties; the Soviet world advocated economic and social rights; the Latin American world concerned itself with the rule of law; the Scandinavians underlined equality between the sexes; India and China stood for non-discrimination, especially in relation to the downtrodden, underdeveloped, and underprivileged, and were also intensely interested in the right to education; others argued for the origin of these rights in the very nature of man itself; those with a dominant religious outlook wanted to safeguard religious freedoms.[4]

Roberto Romulo, Secretary of Foreign Affairs of the Philippines, provides a useful summary of how the developing world views human rights history:

> It is a tragedy that, upon the end of World War II, governments selectively used human rights as ideological weapons or as justification for state policy. They treated human rights in terms of their separate components, instead of as the integrated whole that they are . . . In the West, countries laid almost exclusive emphasis on individual, civil and political rights as an affront to totalitarian adversaries even as they ignored violations of these rights in states politically aligned with them . . . In the East and elsewhere, other nations championed economic, social and cultural rights either as a defensive measure or as justification for their repression of individual and political rights. This occurred at the same time many of them failed to ensure for their own peoples those very same economic, social and cultural rights.[5]

At the time of drafting of the Declaration, it was also thought necessary to create a multilateral treaty which would give legal expression to the assertions in the UDHR. In international law, a treaty represents the strongest form of binding obligation on nations and on their governments. Two international treaties resulted. These treaties became known as the International Covenant on Civil and Political Rights, and the International Covenant on Economic, Social and Cultural Rights.[6] They provide a legal and diplomatic force to human rights which had not previously existed. Once the treatment of individuals within a state is recognized as a matter of international concern, as Ann Kent put it, 'human rights are thus seen as providing a lifebelt between the international community and the individual which by implication bypasses the authority of the state.'[7]

In addition to the general covenants, a regime of more specialized human rights treaties has evolved. This regime includes, for example, prohibitions of torture and degrading punishment, protection of refugees, elimination of discrimination, labour rights, and children's rights. Lack of implementation of these commitments remains a serious problem. As addressed in the following section, problems of enforcement and jurisdiction have plagued the international human rights regime.

Problems of Jurisdiction and Enforcement

The legal relationships between the various human rights instruments discussed above are:

- the human rights provisions of the UN Charter represent legally binding obligations for all UN states;
- parts of the Declaration and the Covenants represent international customary law and are thus binding on all UN states;
- in all other respects, the Covenants, as such, are legally binding only on states which have ratified them; on the signatory states, there is a state responsibility to fulfill the obligations; and
- in addition, these instruments together represent the minimum standard of conduct for all people and all nations.[8]

The principal vehicle for supervision and enforcement of state obligations under the International Covenant on Civil and Political Rights is the UN Human Rights Committee, which consists of eighteen members chosen from the nationals of signatory states. The Covenant imposes an immediate obligation on each signatory to ensure the included rights for all individuals within its territory and subject to its jurisdiction.

The Human Rights Committee receives and examines periodic reports from all signatory states concerning the measures these states have adopted to give effect to the rights and the progress made in their enforcement. The Human Rights Committee's responses to these reports are sent to the reporting states as well as to the UN Economic and Social Council. The main supervision mechanism is, therefore, investigation. The Committee may also receive submissions from non-governmental organizations. Furthermore, a state may declare to the Committee that another state has breached its obligations under the Covenant, provided both states have assumed the specific obligation to allow another signatory to make such a declaration. States are thus liable to answer to adverse publicity and international pressure, which, if fierce enough, may encourage them to take remedial action. However, the Committee has no power to require states to make the periodic reports, nor to change any findings of a reporting state which appear contrary to fact.

The First Optional Protocol to the Covenant allows

individuals in those states which have ratified the protocol to claim that his or her rights under the Covenant have been violated and to make a complaint directly to the Committee after all domestic channels have been exhausted. The Second Optional Protocol prohibits the execution of any person and requires the signatory to abolish the death penalty.[9]

The International Covenant on Economic, Social and Cultural Rights requires a signatory to take steps, individually and through international assistance and co-operation to the maximum of its available resources, progressively to achieve the realization of the rights mentioned in that Covenant. As the obligations imposed are qualified by conditions and are programmatic or goal-directed (rather than strictly enforceable), a different kind of machinery is provided than that of the International Covenant on Civil and Political Rights. States also have to submit periodic reports on their implementation of the treaty, but in this case it is the UN Economic and Social Council which examines the reports. The Council, assisted by eighteen experts, takes the approach that states should be helped to achieve levels of development which make the implementation of these rights possible.

Apart from these two bodies, the UN Commission on Human Rights, established in 1946, mainly investigates complaints that appear to reveal a consistent pattern of gross and reliably attested violations of human rights. However, it cannot enforce its findings; it can merely publicize them.

In 1953, the Western Europeans created a regional structure with the adoption of the European Convention for the Protection of Human Rights and Fundamental Freedoms. The Western European countries felt such a structure was necessary to complement the UN instruments and mechanisms, because the former Soviet bloc was perceived as a growing threat to their values. The structure included a commission and a court which have over the years created a substantial body of law on the interpretation and application of contemporary human rights standards. The Convention has been described as 'the most sophisticated of all contemporary instruments for the international protection of human rights'.[10] This is especially attributed to enforcement mechanisms that allow individuals to bring cases against European governments after exhausting domestic remedies and processes.

Other regional human rights structures followed. The

Organization of American States adopted the American Convention of Human Rights in 1969, which came into force in 1978. The Inter-American Commission is based in Washington, and the Inter-American Court sits in San José, Costa Rica. In 1981, a group of African states adopted the African Charter on Human and Peoples' Rights and ratified it in 1986. The African Charter created the African Commission in 1987.

Asia lags behind the rest of the world in ratifying the International Covenants and in setting up regional human rights mechanisms. One reason for the absence of a regional structure is the wide variety of countries within Asia which includes Japan, India, and Iraq. So far, Asian governments have only agreed to 'explore the possibilities of establishing regional arrangements for the promotion and protection of human rights in Asia'.[11] Discussions so far indicate serious problems in coming up with a conception of human rights both acceptable to Asian governments and agreeable to the outside world.

The Problem of Defining Human Rights

A 'human right' has been defined as 'a conceptual device, expressed in linguistic form, that assigns priority to certain human or social attributes regarded as essential to the adequate functioning of a human being; that is intended to serve as a protective capsule for those attributes; and that appeals for deliberate action to ensure such protection'.[12] Human rights have also been defined as 'the laws and practices that have evolved over the centuries to protect ordinary people, minorities, groups, and races from oppressive rulers and governments',[13] or as 'rights of individuals in society which are regarded as universal and inalienable'.[14]

The Universal Declaration of Human Rights calls for every individual and every government to observe and promote human rights, in the sense that everyone has human rights responsibilities; and it is because of this that these rights can be said to be 'universal'.[15] Further, human rights 'are inalienable, not because they cannot be alienated but because if they are, "the life left is not fully human life".'[16]

Human rights have three effects: to avoid depriving, to protect from depriving, and to aid the deprived. The importance

of human rights is that they are 'simultaneously a prioritiz-
ing, protective and action-demanding concept. . . . In the final
analysis it is not the rights that have special protection but
the attributes they are designed to protect.'[17]

Before the Second World War, the term 'human rights' was
taken to mean civil, and political rights. These rights are
sometimes referred to as 'first generation rights'. Economic,
social, and cultural rights are referred to as 'second generation rights' which have a collective nature. A 'third generation right' came about in 1986 when the right to development
was recognized by the UN Declaration on the Right to
Development. It is now widely advocated that the upholding of human rights is integral to development. The 1986
Declaration recognizes that the human person is the central
subject of development and should be the active participant
and beneficiary of the right to development. It acknowledges
that all human rights are indivisible and interdependent, and
call for equal attention. The Declaration then mandates signatory states to remove 'obstacles' to development arising
from the failure to respect rights and freedom.[18]

The problem of defining human rights lies in the number
and the diversity of rights. Civil rights deal with the individual and do not depend on general social conditions. These
include freedom of thought, expression, association, conscience, religion, residence, and movement. They also include
the right to life and freedom from torture and arbitrary arrest
and detention. Political rights deal with the right to participate in public affairs. These include the right to participate in
free elections under a system of universal and equal suffrage.

Economic rights relate to the right to participate in the
work-force, such as the right to work, to choose freely one's
employment, and to be equally paid for equal work.[19] Social
rights relate to society's claim on the State to a range of services, such as social security, education, and medical care.
The concept of cultural rights is not yet well developed,
although some progress has been made toward protecting
the rights of indigenous peoples.

Other collective rights include the rights of peoples to self-
determination, rights of minorities, development rights, and
environment rights. Self-determination has been further divided into an external and an internal form. External self-
determination refers to the rights of states to determine

national policies, while internal self-determination refers to the rights of peoples within states to choose their form of government. The latter has generally been neglected because of states' fears of secession.

Some have criticized the idea that the concept of human rights should be expanded to cover nearly all human activity. These critics argue that such expansion renders the concept meaningless. As a report by the government of the Netherlands opined, human rights 'no longer indicates minimum conditions for an existence worthy of human dignity, but is beginning to include practically everything which is considered desirable for human development'.[20] Such criticisms are perhaps inevitable in view of the fact that there is a need to encompass and reconcile a variety of views reflected by different political philosophies and systems.

Despite these problems, 'No one now objects to the category "human rights" on the grounds that the level of actual protection of those rights in many countries remains problematic, that the machinery for their protection remains embryonic, or that there are still important areas of uncertainty about the content and application of those rights. These things may be true, but they are taken either as reasons for improving the articulation and enforcement of international human rights standards, or at least as inevitable concomitants, in a diverse, disorganized, and disorderly international community, of recognizing human rights at all.'[21]

The relationship between international human rights and individual human rights under national legal systems is that international law is implemented largely by national law and institutions. Measures for domestic implementation of civil and political rights include providing constitutional protection of human rights; establishing administrative enforcement agencies, such as an ombudsman; holding pluralistic and periodic elections of the legislature; and providing genuine separation of powers, an independent judiciary, and some form of legal aid to enable equal access to justice.

Governments have more discretion as to the choice of means to implement economic, social, and cultural rights. The promotion and protection of these rights do not require any particular structure of government, such as a centrally planned one, or a welfare state. Protection could be provided by the private sector. However, governments have the ultimate responsibility for promotion and protection. It is only when national laws and institutions are deficient that international law comes into play.

This question of ultimate responsibility for implementing human rights was a significant concern of Asian governments in the debate that ensued in the Vienna process. Asian governments essentially sought shelter in sovereignty from international interference in their human rights practices. It is the main contention of the present essay that states should not be allowed to shelter human rights abuse behind the screen of sovereignty and non-interference. It is in this regard that the debates of the Vienna process are considered in the following section.

The Vienna Process

A series of regional preparatory meetings were held prior to the full meeting of the UN World Conference on Human Rights in Vienna. The African Preparatory Meeting was held in Tunis from 2 November to 6 November 1992, and the Latin American and the Caribbean Preparatory Meeting was held in San José, Costa Rica, from 18 January to 22 January 1993. Both meetings produced their respective regional declarations.[22]

However, what became the main source of international contention was the Bangkok Declaration drafted by the representatives of the Asian governments which met in Bangkok from 29 March to 2 April 1993. Claiming to be expressing the 'aspirations and commitments of the Asian region', the signatories of the Bangkok Declaration went on to say, 'all countries, large and small, have the right to determine their political systems, control and freely utilize their resources, and freely pursue their economic, social and cultural development.' They added, 'while human rights are universal in nature, they must be considered in the context of a dynamic and evolving process of international norm-setting, bearing in mind the significance of national and regional particularities and various historical, cultural and religious backgrounds.'[23] This latter phrase was emphasized by those who supported (as well as those who opposed) the Declaration, while the assertions of universality and dynamic norm-setting have been given little regard. Lee Kuan Yew, the Senior Minister of

Singapore, described the Asian view as 'a serious alternative formulation . . . with a different emphasis'.[24]

In other words, standards may vary from place to place. But whose standards are we talking about? Think for a moment of Wei Jingsheng, who spent nearly fifteen years in a Chinese jail for the crime of publishing a newsletter advocating democracy, or Aung Saan Soo Kyi, who is under house arrest in Burma for her liberal political views. Should they be faulted for having failed to appreciate the 'national and regional particularities' of their respective countries? Torture does not hurt less depending on the 'historical, cultural and religious backgrounds' of the person to whose body it is applied.

The Bangkok Declaration further affirmed 'the principles of respect for national sovereignty and territorial integrity as well as non-interference in the internal affairs of States, and the non-use of human rights as an instrument of political pressure'. Though these statements were couched in terms of general rights of countries and states, in fact, the signatories to the Bangkok Declaration sought mainly to assert the rights of government, and to undermine, in doing so, the presumption that an infringement of human rights was also a breach of international law. Whether international law regarding human rights has been breached is not for an accused state to determine finally. Furthermore, as Lewis Henkin wrote, 'if human rights were always a matter of domestic jurisdiction and never a proper subject of external attention in any form,' provisions of the UN Charter, the Universal Declaration of Human Rights, the various international instruments, and the actions of the UN, 'would be *ultra virus*'.[25]

To uphold cultural pluralism is to argue that every culture is equally valid and that no external values should be allowed to influence them. If the argument that cultural, social, or religious factors give rise to different and yet equally valid conceptions of human rights is accepted, then the most despicable acts, such as the mass murder of a class or section of citizens by a government, could be excused under the pretext of cultural pluralism and/or sovereign right.

For example, apartheid could be explained away as a case of the previous South African government exercising 'the right to determine its political system' and 'pursue economic, social and cultural development' of its own very singular and unpleasant kind. Indeed, Article 7 of the Teheran Proclamation specifically condemned apartheid 'as a crime against humanity'. Economic sanctions against South Africa were widely supported. The sanctions were, moreover, supported by several signatories of the Bangkok Declaration, who did not regard them as interfering with the 'internal affairs of states' when applied to someone else.

On another front, the Bangkok Declaration also argued in favour of 'the interdependence and indivisibility of economic, social, cultural, civil, and political rights, and the need to give equal emphasis to all categories of human rights', as well as 'the right to development as a universal and inalienable right and an integral part of fundamental rights.' The Declaration then calls upon the UN to 'discourage any attempt to use human rights as a condition of extending development assistance'.

In discussing economic rights, former US President Jimmy Carter argued that poorer countries have a right to assistance from richer countries.[26] But, by the same token, national governments should not willfully deny economic rights to their own citizens. Economic development is desirable and economic aid should be promoted. But those national governments that would argue that economic rights are indivisible from civil and political rights lose credibility if they themselves are sustaining, through their own ideology, incompetence, or corruption, the very poverty they claim to deplore.

If the Bangkok Declaration was implying that economic rights mean that everybody has a right to be well-off, and that until those rights are satisfied, then other human rights can go unsatisfied as well, then its signatories were being cynical to the extreme. It would appear that there was also an element of moral blackmail directed at the international community. The Bangkok Declaration thus attempted to provide a means for poor and oppressive governments to claim that their styles of government are necessitated by their condition of poverty, while arguing that the only way of inducing them to permit improved human rights is through economic aid from wealthier countries.

Democracy and Human Rights

The Vienna Conference itself was dominated by the confrontation between two conflicting beliefs: the 'universal' concept of human rights championed by the liberal democratic developed world and by non-governmental organizations from around the world; and the 'Asian' concept embodied in the Bangkok Declaration, championed by Asian governments.

The 'Asian view' was developed and forcefully advocated by representatives of China and Singapore.[27] Liu Huaqiu, the Chinese Vice-Foreign Minister, said:

> The concept of human rights is the product of historical development, it is closely associated with specific social, political and economic conditions and with the specific history, culture and values of a particular country. Different historical development stages have different human rights requirements. . . . There are no absolute individual rights and freedoms, except those prescribed by law and within the framework of law. Nobody shall place his own rights and interests above those of the state and society. . . . Each and every Chinese citizen . . . enjoys genuine democracy and freedom, civil and political rights, as well as extensive economic, social and cultural rights.[28]

Wong Kan Seng, Foreign Minister of Singapore, added:

> The extent and exercise of rights, in particular civil rights, varies greatly from one culture or political community to another. . . . All cultures aspire to promote human rights in their own way. But the hard core of rights that are truly universal is perhaps smaller than we sometimes like to pretend. . . . There is already evidence that at some stage an excessive emphasis on individual rights becomes counterproductive.[29]

It is significant that the Bangkok Declaration was silent on the right of citizens to choose their government through free and fair elections. The promoters of the Bangkok Declaration regard 'democracy' as purely a Western concept, unsuitable for realization in Asia. Lee Kwan Yew argues that 'Asia has never valued the individual over society. The society has always been more important than the individual. . . . Human rights standards, as distinct from democracy as a form of government, will become universal. It will not be Western standards, because the West is but a minority of the world.'[30]

The core idea of 'democracy' is rule by the people. The idea has two principles. The first is that of popular control over the process of decision-making. In a direct democracy, as in the Swiss cantons, the people exercise this control of the government themselves. In most cases, however, popular control over the decision-makers is exercised through a representative system. The second principle is that of political equality: all citizens should have equal control, as with citizens' equality before the law. Citizens should share equal rights and each elector's vote should carry the same weight. As stated by David Beetham in a report on democracy in Britain, 'The first principle is underpinned by the value that we give to people as self-determining agents who should have a say on issues that affect their lives; the second is by the assumption that everyone has an equal capacity for self-determination, and therefore, an equal right to influence collective decisions, and to have their interests considered when they are made.'[31]

Asian governments appear to fear democracy because it is perceived to make the job of governing less effective. Perhaps the problem lies in the definition of 'strong' government. It cannot mean a government should be allowed to impose whatever policies it likes as quickly as possible. It cannot mean a government is always right about what it wants to do. Neither does democracy

> mean whatever the people may decide at any given moment; rather it describes a set of rules and procedures for securing their control over decision making or decision makers on an ongoing basis. . . . If elected politicians are ineffective because they lack the powers to deliver their agenda, a loss of confidence in the electoral process is likely to result. On the other hand, key democratic features, such as open government, parliamentary scrutiny and procedures of consultation, all help to make government effective.[32]

The most fundamental citizens' right of all is the right of citizens to reject a government and choose another. All other rights flow from that possibility. True representative government cannot properly function without associated civil freedoms, including those of expression and association, nor can it properly function without the rule of law.

Also at the heart of the human rights debate is style of government. Article 21 of the Universal Declaration of Human Rights states,

> Everyone has the right to take part in the government of his country, directly or through freely chosen representatives. . . . The will of the people shall be the basis of the authority of government; this will shall be expressed in

periodic and genuine elections which shall be by universal and equal suffrage and shall be held by secret vote or by equivalent free voting procedures.

By asserting the powers of government at the expense of the rights of the citizens, the Bangkok Declaration's view of human rights is profoundly undemocratic. It presumes that every government is a just government, a wise government, and a legitimate government. It finds little or no place for the notion that government can be incompetent or wrong and that citizens should be free to reject one government and choose another through the orderly processes of the ballot box. Fortunately the Bangkok proposals were not endorsed in the final Vienna Declaration.

The Vienna Declaration and Programme for Action

The Vienna Declaration and Programme for Action, issued on the last day of the Conference, produced a compromise statement on universality and cultural pluralism:

> All human rights are universal, indivisible and inter-dependent and inter-related. The international community must treat human rights globally in a fair and equal manner, on the same footing, and with the same emphasis. While the significance of national and regional particularities and various historical, cultural and religious backgrounds must be borne in mind, it is the duty of states, regardless of their political, economic and cultural systems, to promote and protect human rights and fundamental freedoms.
>
> Democracy, development, and respect for human rights and fundamental freedoms are inter-dependent and mutually reinforcing. . . . While development facilitates the enjoyment of human rights, the lack of development may not be invoked to justify the abridgement of internationally recognized human rights.[33]

Non-government organizations (NGOs) did not regard the various compromises as a triumph. Amnesty International saw the debate as just repeating old arguments: 'no radically new principles have been articulated to address the enormous challenges of today's world and to move the Universal Declaration of Human Rights from a "common standard of achievement" to an "obligation under international law". The text does not even state that human rights violations are an obstacle to development.' The references to national and regional particularities were seen as weakening the concept of universality.[34]

Furthermore, Amnesty International and other NGOs strongly encouraged the UN to elevate the human rights issue by creating the position of UN High Commissioner for Human Rights. The establishment of this post could not be agreed in Vienna but the issue was taken up again later in the year by the UN General Assembly. The post was finally established in December of 1993. The Commissioner is the UN official with principal responsibility for UN human rights activities under the direction and authority of the Secretary-General. The first Commissioner is José Ayala Lasso, a diplomat who was previously Bolivia's envoy to the UN. The human rights community appears to be happy that the Commissioner has been willing to be involved in crisis situations, including making public statements concerning the situation in Rwanda, but it is too early to assess how successful he will be in resolving conflicts. The fear is that, burdened with diplomatic squabbles and red tape he will become ineffective. The other problem is that his annual budget is inadequate.

The fact that the Vienna Conference took place at all reflected a desire on the part of the UN member states to portray themselves publicly as caring about human rights, whatever the underlying reality. But, Ibrahim Fall, Assistant Secretary-General for Human Rights and Secretary-General of the Conference, warned of the dangers of empty rhetoric, saying: 'History will judge us, not by words on the pages of this Declaration, but by the sincerity of our efforts and the success we achieve' in changing the way people live. 'The credibility of the whole United Nations is at stake.'[35]

The Vienna Declaration, by elevating all individual and collective rights to the same level, must, as an absolute minimum, mean that these rights, and whatever measures are necessary to secure their realization, are non-negotiable. As Philip Alston explained, 'That is not to say that there is not enormous room for debate as to the best policies for achieving the desired objectives, but simply that the objectives themselves are not open to refutation on economic rationalist or other grounds.'[36] As discussed in the following section, international non-governmental organizations played a significant role in this process by promoting a firm stand on human rights.

Non-Governmental Organizations

For non-governmental organizations the international human rights movement can be said to have reached maturity when Amnesty International was awarded the Nobel Prize for Peace in 1977. In the 1980s, several new internationally focused specialist organizations, such as the Lawyers Committee for Human Rights, Article 19, and the Committee to Protect Journalists added their strength to the movement. Michael Posner of the Lawyers Committee for Human Rights has characterized this role as follows:

> By providing accurate, objective and up-to-date information about human rights abuses they have effectively transformed the UN's debate. They have also pressed for a more open agenda, for increased participation . . . at UN meetings, and for the UN to live up to its commitments to protect and promote respect for human rights. . . . Many governments have resisted NGO participation in the UN at every turn. In particular, those governments that are themselves gross human rights violators have quickly realized that human rights NGOs are much more likely to expose their violations publicly than other governments would be.[37]

This was clearly the case at Vienna.[38] Non-governmental organizations spoke out for the victims of abuses, while the official delegates debated their governments' respective philosophies. China and some other governments tried, and had some success with, limiting the access of these organizations to the conference. They vetoed their attendance at sessions to draft the Vienna Declaration and sought to strip accreditation from those organizations they found most irksome, such as those which were formed by dissidents abroad after 4 June 1989, those with strong concerns about the Tiananmen Massacre.

Vienna also witnessed the strength of local human rights organizations. Representatives came from many countries, ranging from wealthy Japan to struggling Mongolia. Despite vastly different backgrounds and experiences, there was a remarkable willingness to organize and to delegate the lobbying work that needed to be done. Organizations from the Asia-Pacific Region were particularly active in working against the spirit of the Bangkok Declaration. Although the Bangkok Declaration found no support among Asian or other organizations, they did seem to feel that Asian and other developing-world views should be heard on human rights issues. The time had come, they agreed, for a more equal relationship between the established international non-governmental organizations of the West, and the local organizations of the developing world.

The growth of more powerful and assertive developing-world organizations clearly is to be welcomed as a major contribution towards the protection of human rights. Indigenous human rights movements by their mere existence refute the claim by many of their governments that such rights are foreign concepts. Their activities cannot be dismissed as foreign meddling in the internal affairs of a country. Likewise their campaigns enjoy a greater chance for success because they would be more attuned to the political processes and public sensitivities of their respective nations.

At least in the near term, however, the work of local organizations will remain difficult and sometimes dangerous, even though the Vienna Declaration acknowledged the role of these groups as crucial to the creation of 'favorable conditions at national, regional and international levels'. Many governments of the developing world view human rights groups with suspicion, disapproval, or even outright hostility. Many activists run great personal risks, even though they are often seeking only to have their governments honour and enforce the declarations and covenants these same governments have signed. Although these organizations can help one another by building on the solidarity experienced in Vienna, they also need the support of other governments and citizens around the world. Effective domestic implementation of human rights law depends in large part on the ability of these groups to survive and flourish.

The UN could adopt the following measures to better secure the survival of non-governmental organizations:

• The UN should urge member states to take whatever actions necessary to enable NGOs to operate freely.

• UN departments and agencies should strengthen contacts with NGOs.

• Groups should be allowed to participate more meaningfully in international meetings such as the Vienna Conference. This should include being granted access to formal meetings and being provided with the necessary documentation in order to work effectively. Written and oral interventions should be allowed.

• Immediate steps should be taken to end the distinction between international and local groups; all groups should be eligible to file reports with the UN Economic and Social Council.

It has also been suggested that the UN should prepare and publish a report on the situation and treatment of human rights organizations:

> Such a report could be prepared by an independent expert . . . [and] should assess the laws and practices in every member state with respect to these groups. . . . The report should contain recommendations on ways in which the rights of non-governmental organizations and human rights advocates to operate freely can be strengthened, particularly in the national context. The report should be updated on a periodic basis.[39]

Conclusion

The UN Charter, the Universal Declaration Human Rights, and the various UN human rights instruments remain generally unknown and unrealized for hundreds of millions of members of the human family. Many UN members and signatories to the various human rights treaties have done little to build a human rights culture in their own countries. Intensive public education is sorely needed.

The whole logic of human rights is based upon the principle that all human beings are possessed of an equal worth and dignity. Not only is the principle of 'universality' being inadequately practised and applied, it is also being openly disputed by governments advocating cultural pluralism and sovereignty. Those who do so plead, in effect, for the extension of state power; yet the balance of power is already tilted overwhelmingly in favour of the state. It is the rights of the individual, and the rights of minorities, that need to be reinforced.

The Universal Declaration of Human Rights and the International Covenants provide a moral and legal framework for freeing the individual from terror and oppression and, eventually, also from poverty and want. It can only damage the individual citizen if governments try to play civil and political rights off against economic, social, and cultural rights, while failing to deliver on either. Collective and individual rights are but two sides of a single coin. As individuals, we should extend to others across society precisely those rights which we would wish others to extend to us.

Any form of 'development' worthy of that name must involve education, democracy, and human rights. Repression is not a means to economic development. Respect for human rights is not an obstacle to economic growth, and is, indeed, a precondition for sustaining it. Development is a legitimate expectation, but it is never an acceptable excuse for failing to respect other human rights.

The developed-world has made forthright commitments to the international promotion of human rights through their foreign policies, sometimes including their development aid programs. In reality, however, actions they have taken, or refrained from taking on human rights grounds, have often been politically selective rather than principled and consistent. Unless policies are credible and consistent, they will continue to be viewed by the developing world as the assertion of cultural superiority and moral condescension.

The standing organ of the UN, the Security Council, is mandated to address situations which threaten international peace and security, but it is reluctant to see itself as having a human rights mandate. As long as the governments which make up the Security Council continue to act selectively rather than out of principles, only limited changes can be expected in the foreseeable future.

The most positive development has been the growing assertiveness of human rights NGOs over the past two decades. In the final analysis, it is the capacity of individuals and groups to be concerned and moved by injustice that is the real driving force behind the human rights movement.

Notes

1. Hersch Lauterpacht, cited in James Avery Joyce, *The New Politics of Human Rights*, New York: St Martin's Press, 1976.
2. John P. Humphreys, 'The World Revolution and Human Rights', in A. E. Gottlieb (ed.), *Human Rights, Federalism and Minorities*, Toronto: Canadian Institute of International Affairs, 1970, cited in Nihal Jayawickrama, 'Hong Kong and International Protection of Human Rights', in Raymond Wacks (ed.), *Human Rights in Hong Kong*, Hong Kong: Oxford University Press, 1992, pp. 120–75.
3. Sandra Burton, 'Society versus the Individual', Interview with Lee Kwan Yew, *Time*, 14 June 1993, p. 21.
4. Address to the opening session of the Conference on Non-governmental Organizations, in Observance of the 25th Anniversary of the Universal Declaration of Human Rights, UN Headquarters, New York, 10 December 1993, cited in Jayawickrama, 'Hong Kong and International Protection of Human Rights'.
5. Roberto Romulo, *Far Eastern Economic Review*, 12 August 1993, p. 24.
6. International Covenant on Civil and Political Rights, 21 *UN GAOR. Supp.* (No. 16) 52, 6 *I.L.M.* 368(1967); International Covenant on Economic, Social and Cultural Rights, 21 *UN GAOR. Supp.* (No. 16)49, 6 *I.L.M.* 360 (1967). As of 31 December 1992, 115 countries had ratified the International Covenant on Civil and Political Rights, with 67 also ratifying the First Optional Protocol, 11 the Second Optional Protocol, and 114 countries ratified the International Covenant on Economic, Social and Cultural Rights. *Amnesty International Report* ,1993 (London: Amnesty International Publications, 1993).
7. Ann Kent, *Between Freedom and Subsistence — China and Human Rights*, Hong Kong: Oxford University Press, 1993.
8. B. G. Ramcharan, *The Concept and Present Status of International Protection of Human Rights: Forty Years After the Universal Declaration*, Dordrecht, The Netherlands: Martinus Nijhoff Publishers, 1989.
9. The First Optional Protocol came into force in March 1976 and the Second Optional Protocol in December 1989.
10. John P. Humphrey, 'The International Law of Human Rights in the Middle Twentieth Century', in Maarten Bos (ed.), *The Present State of International Law and other Essays*, Kluwer, The Netherlands: Deventer, 1973.
11. Bangkok Declaration, Art. 26
12. Michael Freeden, *Rights*, Miton Keynes: Open University Press, 1991.

13. Charles Humana, *World Human Rights Guide,* 3rd edn., New York: Oxford University Press, 1992.
14. Kent, *Between Freedom and Subsistence — China and Human Rights.*
15. Joyce, *The New Politics of Human Rights.*
16. R. J. Vincent, *Human Rights and International Relations,* Cambridge: Cambridge University Press, 1986.
17. Freeden, *Rights.*
18. UN Declaration on the Rights to Development 4 December 1986, G.A. Res. 41/128, *Y.B.U.N.,* 40 (1986): 717. The UN Declaration on the Right to Development (1986) recognizes in Art. 2.1 that the human person is the central subject of development and should be the active participant and beneficiary of the right to development. It is not open to governments, therefore, to argue that the rights of individuals might have to be compromised for the sake of development. It should also be noted that at the Earth Summit, held at Rio de Janeiro in 1992, inter-relations and tensions between the environment and economic development were debated. The right to development must now be seen to mean the right to 'sustainable' development.
19. Until recently, the US sought to characterize economic, social and cultural rights as 'goals' or 'aspirations' but not as human rights. The US signed the ICCPR and the ICESCR during the Carter Administration, but the ICCPR was only ratified by the US Congress in 1992 during the Bush Administration. The Clinton Administration has now undertaken to ratify the ICESCR in the near future.
20. Government of the Netherlands, *Human Rights and Foreign Policy,* The Hague, 1979.
21. J. Crawford, *The Rights of Peoples: Some Conclusions,* cited in Kent, *Between Freedom and Subsistence — China and Human Rights.*
22. Western European and other states did not hold regional meetings.
23. Japan's delegate to the Bangkok Preparatory Meeting, Seiichiro Otsuke, recorded the Japanese Government's many reservations to the Bangkok Declaration. 'Japan', he said, 'believes that human rights should not be sacrificed for development.'
24. Burton, 'Society versus the Individual'.
25. Lewis Henken, *The Age of Rights,* New York: Columbia University Press, 1990.
26. Jimmy Carter, former President of the US, Address to Vienna Conference on 14 June 1993.
27. Neither China nor Singapore have acceded to either of the international human rights covenants discussed above.
28. Liu Huaqiu, Address to the Vienna Conference on 15 June 1993.
29. Wong Ken Sang, Address to the Vienna Conference on 16 June 1993.

30. Burton, 'Society versus the Individual'.
31. The Democratic Audit of the United Kingdom, Auditing Democracy in Britain, Compiled by David Beetham, London: Charter 88 Trust, 1992.
32. *Ibid.*
33. United Nations World Conference on Human Rights: Vienna Declaration and Programme of Action, adopted 25 June 1993, 32 I.L.M. 1661, 1993.
34. *Amnesty International Report* (Annual Report), 1993.
35. Ibrahim Fall's closing remarks, Vienna Conference, 25 June 1993.
36. Philip Alston, 'Importance of the Inter-Play between Economic, Social and Cultural Rights, and Civil and Political Rights', *Human Rights at the Dawn of the 21st Century*, Interregional meetings organized by the Council of Europe in advance of the World Conference on Human Rights, Council of Europe Press, 1993.
37. Michael H. Posner, 'The Establishment of Rights of Non-governmental Human Rights Groups to Operate', New York: Lawyers Committee for Human Rights, June 1993.
38. According to the 'Final Meeting and Roundup' issued by the UN Information Center on 28 June 1993, more than 3,000 representatives of 813 NGOs attended the Conference, outnumbering the approximately 2,100 government representatives.
39. Posner, 'The Establishment of Rights of Non-governmental Human Rights Groups to Operate'.

Adopting International Standards of Human Rights in Hong Kong

Michael Davis

Any employment of the concept of human rights, and consequently any attempt to draft human rights legislation, is in the present age an exercise in comparative law in which international standards, practices, and values inevitably play a role. As this book has explored the concept of human rights both in international and Chinese practice, it is useful to consider a context, such as Hong Kong, where these two traditions converge. The concept of human rights as we know it is rooted in the Age of Enlightenment and notions of social contract. This concept took root in the Constitution of the United States in its Bill of Rights and in France in the Declaration of the Rights of Man. With these roots, bills of rights, which have been included in constitutions around the world, while often varied in content, have generally been the products of borrowings from other contexts and legal traditions. Hong Kong, the subject of the present essay, is an especially good example of this tradition of comparison and borrowing. This essay discusses the pervasive international influences in this particular Asian attempt to secure human rights. The international perspective serves to illustrate how the discursive model, discussed earlier in this book, may operate at the local level in a reasonably developed legal system.

The Hong Kong Bill of Rights, enacted in June of 1991, and Hong Kong's evolving concept of human rights, are good examples of this tradition of borrowing and adaptation. That Hong Kong's human rights legislation and practices are seeds planted in Asian soil is of special interest in the present inquiry. An examination of this seeding process illustrates how implementing human rights, particularly in Asia, inevitably submerges a community in a complex web of international principles and practices. Once international principles and practices are so intricately and completely implicated, the attraction of universal standards becomes, in the present age, almost magnetic as increasing demands are made.

For politically developing communities such as Hong Kong,

the level of engagement with international discourse and practices may be even more substantial than that in older more established systems. Older systems, such as that of the United States, while often a source of human right ideas, tend to be more insular and less prone to reception of outside influences. Hong Kong, on the other hand, is endeavouring to build a human rights regime, practically from scratch, by borrowing heavily from outside experience.

The Hong Kong Bill of Rights and Hong Kong's emerging human rights picture, while rooted in Hong Kong's colonial experience, can be viewed as a direct product of the Sino-British Joint Declaration, which returns Hong Kong to Chinese sovereignty in 1997.[1] While under common law Hong Kong had enjoyed certain human rights protections, this tradition had not been codified in any meaningful way, though Britain had acceded to the international human rights covenants on Hong Kong's behalf.[2] Under these covenants Britain has been obligated to conform Hong Kong laws to the treaty requirements and to report periodically concerning compliance.

The Joint Declaration, while assuring maintenance of Hong Kong's current economic and social systems, guarantees the application of a long list of human rights and requires that the 'provisions of the International Covenant on Civil and Political Rights and the International Covenant on Economic, Social and Cultural Rights as applied to Hong Kong shall remain in force.'[3] At the same time, in Joint Declaration Annex I, Article XI, the Chinese government assumed the obligation to implement fully these international covenants to which China is not a party. This presumably includes the above implementation and reporting requirements. Although China argues to the contrary, for the Chinese to fail to give such reports after 1997 would be a breach of the Joint Declaration's requirement to implement those covenants 'as applied to Hong Kong'.

Signing the Joint Declaration set the stage for massive efforts by both the Chinese and British governments to implement these guarantees. This also set the stage for the confrontation and convergence of varied human rights traditions to produce the hybrid that is emerging in Hong Kong. International influences are pervasive.

Lest anyone doubt that this Hong Kong hybrid can thrive in the Asian soil in which it is planted, they need only consider Hong Kong's rich human rights debate of recent months. This debate included a number of claims highlighting the Sino-British failure to localize fully the laws; noting a Sino-British breach of Basic Law requirements concerning the make-up of the future highest court of appeals; attacking plans by the Chinese governments to establish a provisional legislature, and attacking the present government's failure to present legislation to establish a human rights commission or tribunal. This debate is even more striking when one considers that Hong Kong is a Chinese community which has only recently awakened to its political task.

Human rights groups have emphasized the needs for more education on human rights, for an independent human rights tribunal, for an independent legal aid agency, for alteration of the loser-pays-all cost rules for cases brought to protect human rights, for the extension of more international human rights conventions to Hong Kong, for protection of the press, for ensuring judicial independence, and for ensuring post-1997 reporting under the applicable human rights covenants.[4] Some leading figures in the pro-China camp and Chinese officials have criticized the Bill of Rights and other human rights initiatives. At the same time they have sought to promote greater awareness of the Basic Law. A look at the constitutional foundation for this debate is instructive.

An International Constitutional Framework

The Sino-British Joint Declaration

The 1984 Sino-British Joint Declaration appears to put the future Hong Kong Special Administrative Region squarely within a liberal, capitalist, common law framework. Not only does the Joint Declaration guarantee a plethora of rights associated with the liberal tradition, but it also aims to ensure judicial enforcement in the common law tradition, along with various associated democratic and capitalist elements. The rights to be protected include the standard litany of rights and freedoms, 'including those of the person, of speech, of the press, of assembly, of association, of travel, of movement, of correspondence, of strike, of choice of occupation, of academic research and of religious belief. . . .'[5] Various property, due process, and democratic rights are also assured. The liberal commitment of these guarantees is evident in the fact that over half of the enumerated rights relate to some aspect of freedom of expression.

Not only are the rights liberally enumerated, but the Joint Declaration also assures maintenance of the common law system for their implementation. This and other related assurances promises a strong commitment to the rule of law. The Joint Declaration provides that the common law system will be maintained, that the Basic Law — to be enacted in accordance with the agreement — will be the supreme law, and that people 'shall have the right to challenge the actions of the executive in the courts'.[6] These various guarantees promise a vigorous commitment to human rights and the rule of law.

The Hong Kong Basic Law

The Joint Declaration stipulates that the terms of this promise be enacted in a Basic Law. The Basic Law was enacted by the National People's Congress (NPC) in April 1990 after a lengthy consultation and drafting process.[7] While generally containing the provisions stipulated in the Joint Declaration, the Basic Law, in key areas, marks some retreat from the guarantees of the agreement. Certain contrary characteristics of the Chinese constitutional tradition emerged as prevalent themes in the final Basic Law.

Most striking in this regard was the retreat on the democracy front. The historical Chinese concern with the alleged instability of popular democracy was evident. The Joint Declaration's promise that the legislature would be 'constituted by elections' became, in the Basic Law, a system of minority politics made up largely of legislators selected by functional constituencies (i.e. selected industries, labour, and other sectors) and some initial election committee participation whose members also would be selected by functional sectors. The Joint Declaration's guarantee of selecting the Chief Executive 'by election or through consultations' became fully an election committee system, with electors on the committee again coming from functional sectors.[8]

Another marked retreat from the spirit of the Joint Declaration is evident in provisions in the Basic Law that are designed to strengthen the central government's ability to control public order directly and to restrict foreign intrusion in Hong

Kong's affairs. The former includes Article 18 which allows the Standing Committee of the NPC to issue an order applying the relevant national laws to the Region if China 'decides to declare a state of war or, by reason of turmoil . . . [within the Region] which endangers national unity or security and is beyond the control of the government of the Region. . . .' The latter aims particularly at restricting the political participation of local residents with foreign rights of abode and inhibiting 'foreign political organizations or bodies from conducting political activities in the Region' or local organizations from 'establishing ties' with such foreign organizations.[9] The addition of these provisions to the final version of the Basic Law followed on the heels of the tragic events at Tiananmen on 4 June 1989.

Otherwise, with some restraint on the part of the future Chinese government, the Basic Law could prove to contain a reasonably usable commitment to human rights. Of course this conditional element of restraint is critical to any human rights regime. After much vacillation and several much less acceptable drafts, the final *draft* Basic Law, published in February of 1989, reduced the viable avenues for restricting human rights. This improved language remained unaltered in the final Basic Law promulgated in April of 1990. While earlier drafts had articulated a conditional human rights regime with numerous grounds for restriction, the final Basic Law, like the February 1989 draft, appears to require that any restrictions prescribed by law meet the requirements of 'the International Covenant on Civil and Political Rights, the International Covenant on Economic, Social and Cultural Rights, and international labour conventions as applied to Hong Kong'.[10] These guarantees are of course subject to interpretation.

The question concerning the interpretation of the Basic Law was a major area of contention in the drafting process. Chinese reluctance to trust the courts with a constitutional judicial review function was in evidence as mainland drafters, who were in the majority on the drafting committee, sought to incorporate language which would place the power to review Hong Kong's laws entirely in the hands of the Standing Committee of the National People's Congress.[11] China, historically depreciating the role of courts and resisting the rule of law, employs a system of legislative interpretation of its constitution.[12] The final model for interpretation adopted in the Hong Kong Basic Law is a hybrid of the Chinese system of legislative interpretation, the civil law constitutional practice of employing a constitutional court or committee, and the common law tradition of vesting the power of interpretation and review under a written constitution in the ordinary courts.

Article 158 of the Basic Law provides that the power of interpretation be vested in the Standing Committee of the NPC but provides that the Standing Committee shall authorize the courts of the Special Administrative Region (SAR) 'to interpret on their own, in adjudicating cases, the provisions of this Law which are within the limits of the autonomy of the Region.'[13] In cases involving matters which are the responsibility of the central government or concern the relationship between the central government and the SAR, where such interpretation affects the outcome of the case, courts are required to seek an interpretation from the Standing Committee of the NPC through the SAR Court of Final Appeal before rendering a final non-appealable judgement. The Standing Committee is required to consult its Committee for the Basic Law (which will be made up of an equal number of both Hong Kong and Mainland members) before giving such interpretation. This latter provision clearly violates the requirements of local judicial independence and finality specified in the Joint Declaration.

Article 17 of the Basic Law further provides for the Standing Committee, after consulting the Committee for the Basic Law, to review SAR laws for conformity to the provisions of the Basic Law.[14] This review power is confined to 'affairs within the responsibility of the Central Authorities' or matters respecting local/central government relations. This provision exceeds the related provision in Annex I, Article II of the Joint Declaration which merely provided for the reporting of SAR legislation to the Standing Committee 'for the record'.

Given the above provisions relating to interpretation and the provision for supremacy of the Basic Law, these articles would appear to afford the local courts the power of constitutional review for matters within the scope of local autonomy, though such is not expressly provided. This conclusion is further indicated by the required maintenance of Hong Kong's common law system. Any interpretation of these articles which might deny the local courts the power of constitutional judicial review would impose serious difficulties and would cause the Basic Law to violate related requirements in the Joint Declaration.[15]

Whether or not the human rights provisions in the Basic Law will be successfully implemented depends largely on the extent to which the local courts are vested with interpreting and implementing them. Since China cannot be expected to make implementing human rights standards a priority for Hong Kong, given its own weak record and experience in this area, it will be up to local courts to protect and implement these rights. This is not only required by the Joint Declaration but is also a sensible and prudent way to maintain Hong Kong's autonomy.

Given the importance of the local courts, the make-up of the future Court of Final Appeals, at the local judiciary's pinnacle, will also be very important to the development of Hong Kong's human rights and other jurisprudence. Though the Basic Law permits the appointment of qualified foreign judges to this highest court, as has been Hong Kong's tradition, the Chinese government, in an agreement with Britain, sought to limit such foreign participation to only one member. This proposal is being resisted by the local Bar Association and the Legislative Council.

China's Human Rights Tradition

The prospect of China's NPC Standing Committee attempting directly to assume or interfere with the local judicial review function under the Basic Law is troubling. China's Standing Committee has little useful experience in a judicial role, particularly with regard to human rights, and China's operative concept of human rights runs quite contrary to the liberal capitalist model which is indicated by the Joint Declaration and aims to ensure a successful Hong Kong.

Professors Randle Edwards and Andrew Nathan have identified the distinguishing characteristics of China's tradition as follows: rights are often juxtaposed with citizens' duties, as indicated by the titles of the rights chapters in both the Constitution of the People's Republic of China and the Hong Kong Basic Law; rights are not considered inherent in humanhood, as under natural rights doctrine, but are treated as a creation of the State; the Chinese socialist tradition places greater emphasis on welfare rights and de-emphasizes political rights, as the Chinese government perceives to be necessary in a developing country; instead of rights limiting the State, the State's interest's are often a limit on rights.[16] This characterization of China's rights tradition appears to be borne out by China's description of its own rights tradition in its recent white paper on human rights which emphasized economic developmental concerns, sovereignty, and the preeminence of collective over individual interest as a basis of rights.[17]

In this light, one can question the viability of entrusting the interpretation of Hong Kong's human rights tradition to a Mainland political body. It would be much better entrusted to a local judiciary made up of the most qualified judges steeped in the common law tradition. This area clearly calls for China's restraint. It was with the above in mind, in the aftermath of the crisis at Tiananmen and the concurrent demonstrations in Hong Kong, that Hong Kong's Bill of Rights was developed.

The Hong Kong Bill of Rights

Much like the Basic Law, the Bill of Rights Ordinance[18] enacted in 1991 combines several human rights concepts. As suggested by the above analysis, the context in which it was passed alone does this. The idea of a bill of rights had been discussed both in and outside government before the 1989 crisis. Some felt it was a necessary component of the current law reform being carried out in preparation for the 1997 hand-over. Recent law reform efforts in Hong Kong generally aim at conforming legislation to existing general practice or the emerging ideal.

The government finally submitted bill of rights legislation in response to the local outcry over the massacre of 4 June 1989. The human rights bill was submitted nearly concurrently with the proposal for a new airport and the submission in Britain of the British Nationality Act, all three aiming at a rescue package for a jittery Hong Kong. Under the circumstances, the Chinese government reacted quite negatively to the bill of rights, alleging that it aimed at usurping China's constitutional role in Hong Kong.

The Make-up of the Bill of Rights

The Hong Kong government's response to China's opposition was carefully to adopt the provisions of the International Covenant on Civil and Political Rights 'as applied to Hong Kong' as the language of the Hong Kong Bill of Rights Ordinance. It was alleged that this should eliminate any grounds for objection since adherence to this covenant was required by both the Joint Declaration and the Basic Law.[19] By passing it as an ordinance, the government sought to allay China's fears about constitutional usurpation.

This means that the International Covenant, under the Bill of Rights Ordinance, is not fully entrenched, and that the human rights provisions in this legislation can be amended or abolished by subsequent legislation or even abrogated by China on some asserted constitutional basis (though any such claim would be hard to substantiate). Yet the ordinance is a sort of super-legislation which, in Part (I), not only provides that it overrides all existing laws, but also requires that subsequent legislation should 'be construed as being subject to this ordinance'.

The International Covenant on Civil and Political Rights is, nevertheless, fully entrenched until 1997. To further enhance the attempt to develop Hong Kong's human rights jurisprudence, when the Bill of Rights Ordinance was enacted, the Queen concurrently amended Hong Kong's present constitution. The Letters Patent now provides for direct application on a constitutional level of the International Covenant 'as applied to Hong Kong'.[20] Unlike the Bill of Rights Ordinance, which can remain in force after 1997, this latter provision will expire on 1 July 1997 along with the Letters Patent.

In the meantime, Hong Kong can develop human rights jurisprudence under the Bill of Rights Ordinance and through the exercise of constitutional judicial review under the International Covenant on Civil and Political Rights incorporated in the Letters Patent. China would be well advised to allow the Bill of Rights Ordinance to remain in place after the transition and to take advantage of this developed jurisprudence to facilitate a smooth transition under similar constitutional guarantees in the Basic Law.

In addition to the convergence of the objectives of the Basic Law and the Bill of Rights Ordinance noted above, it is important to note that the Bill of Rights Ordinance represents a convergence of various forces for human rights. The International Covenant on Civil and Political Rights, which it copies, represents a convergence of the several concepts of human rights that existed at the time it was hammered out by the various developed, developing, and socialist countries.

While the International Covenant, and thus the Bill of Rights Ordinance, contains the usual list of liberal rights (e.g. rights relating to equality, protection of life, prohibition of slavery and torture, protection of liberty, due process of law, privacy, religious belief, freedom of expression, etc.), the generous use of restrictions clauses diminishes this human rights commitment. This is especially true with respect to the restrictions clause employed with the free speech guarantee, which states that the 'exercise of the right . . . carries with it special duties and responsibilities'.[21] Further convergence of varied human rights experiences is becoming evident in the implementation process.

Implementing the Bill of Rights

Given that the requirements of both the amended Letters Patent and the Bill of Rights Ordinance expressly impose on Hong Kong a system of common law judicial review of legislation under a written bill of rights, one would expect significant development of human rights jurisprudence; this has occurred.[22] It also appears that the courts will not hesitate to look beyond Hong Kong for precedent.

In its first exercise of such judicial review of legislation under the Bill of Rights, the Hong Kong Court of Appeals, in *R. v. Sin Yau-ming* (Silke V.P.), expressed the general view that the Bill of Rights Ordinance should be interpreted in a broad and generous manner, stating:

> While this court is, in effect, required to make new Hong Kong law relating to the manner of interpretation of the Hong Kong Bill and consequentially the tests to be applied to those laws now existing and, when asked, those laws yet to be enacted, we are not without guidance in our task. This can be derived from decisions taken in common law jurisdictions which contain a constitutionally entrenched Bill of Rights. We can also be guided by decisions of the European Court of Human Rights — 'the European Court' — and the European Human Rights Commission — 'the

Commission'. Further, we can bear in mind the comments and decisions of the United Nations Human Rights Committee — 'the Committee'. I would hold none of these to be binding upon us though in so far as they reflect the interpretation of articles in the Covenant, and are directly related to Hong Kong legislation, I would consider them as of the greatest assistance and give to them considerable weight. The approach of those bodies differs from that of a domestic court whose task is to determine the constitutionality or otherwise of domestic legislation measured, as is the case in Hong Kong, against an entrenched instrument. So they are helpful but not always apposite.

Greater assistance can be derived from those two common law jurisdictions, the United States of America and Canada, which have constitutionally entrenched bills of rights. The American Bill of Rights is, of course, of lineage far older than either the International Covenant on Civil and Political Rights or the European Covenant — which predates the Covenant by some 175 years — and is embodied in the Constitution of the United States and its Amendments.[23]

In discussing the case, which involved the constitutionality of legislation embodying a presumption of guilt, the Court noted that Canadian jurists 'have looked to the United States for much of the jurisprudential basis for the construction of the Canadian Charter'.

Following *Sin Yau-ming*, the Hong Kong courts, in numerous reported Bill of Rights cases, have considered outside precedent, especially under the Canadian Charter and the European Convention on Human Rights. The local courts have been especially busy with Bill of Rights cases relating to criminal law and procedure. The courts have so far shown a somewhat conservative streak, with some reluctance to adopt the more liberal foreign precedent, such as, for example, that embodied in such doctrine as the American exclusionary rule (a rule that provides for the exclusion of improperly obtained evidence).[24] The courts have insisted that relevant Canadian and American cases are only persuasive and not binding authority.[25] Considering Hong Kong courts' decisions to date, it would seem China need not fear excessive activism from the future SAR courts. It should also be noted, however, that this is a two-way street. Having domesticated the international covenant, Hong Kong may contribute to the growing international jurisprudence surrounding international human rights covenants.

Other Human Rights Legislation

While the present developing body of law under the Bill of Rights should facilitate a smooth transition to operation under similar guarantees in the Basic Law after 1997, some weaknesses have appeared. There have been shortcomings in this evolving jurisprudence in the civil context, especially with respect to discrimination. This may be due to the prohibitive cost of bringing such cases under the local 'loser-pays-all' cost system. Further shortcomings are evident with respect to giving citizens open access to government, protecting the press, and developing human rights awareness and expertise at all levels of government. These concerns have spawned legislative proposals, but considerable reluctance to act, particularly from a local government sensitive to China's criticisms. Though legislators have advanced private members' bills in these areas, the Hong Kong government's response to such initiatives has been lukewarm.

The Human Rights and Equal Opportunities Commission Legislation (discussed in Anna Wu's essay) offers an especially useful and less costly way to implement and promote the constitutional guarantees afforded in the Basic Law. It would establish an independent Human Rights and Equal Opportunities Commission to promote and develop human rights and an Equal Opportunities Tribunal as a specialist branch of the judiciary. This legislation, along with other legislative proposals relating to equal opportunities, free access to information, and protection of the press, could go a long way in assuring that Hong Kong achieves the international human rights standards promised in the Joint Declaration and Basic Law in an efficient and cost-effective manner. Unfortunately, the Chinese government has maintained a negative position on all human rights proposals, and the British Hong Kong government has recently refused to push forward with these proposals in the face of such opposition.

A Cross-section of Human Rights Concepts

As Hong Kong moves closer to 1997 the Hong Kong Bill of Rights Ordinance and other human rights legislation could facilitate its smooth transition to local self-rule under the terms of the Joint Declaration and the Basic Law. Rights concerns that are presently a source of considerable anxiety in Hong Kong and China could continue to be addressed through formal legal channels less subject to overt politicization. The Bill of Rights Ordinance has so far afforded Hong Kong the opportunity to benefit from and address a cross-section of experiences and concerns in the human rights area. A Human Rights Commission and other legislative guarantees would only enhance the community's awareness in this regard. If these developmental processes were permitted to go forward before 1997 Hong Kong would be faced with less uncertainty during the critical transition period. Unfortunately, China has sought to foreclose such development and has threatened to set aside all such attempts to secure human rights by legislation.

The recent human rights developments in Hong Kong certainly undercut the argument that universal human rights standards and processes have no application in an Asian context. As the above analysis reveals, Hong Kong's rigorous engagement with international principles of human rights is evident on several levels. These levels are all relevant to understanding and implementing human rights under the Joint Declaration and current world practice.

• *Context*: The human rights debate in Hong Kong has been strongly influenced by contextual factors. In this regard the most profound influence has been the extremely divergent attitudes of China and Hong Kong concerning human rights. This divergence is in many ways responsible for the creation of the concept of the Hong Kong model of 'one country, two systems'. Given the fundamental differences in the parties' views toward all aspects of human rights, confidence in Hong Kong's future will require mutual understanding and a willingness by China, as the senior partner in this arrangement, to allow Hong Kong to implement the human rights commitments of the Joint Declaration.

• *Sources*: The sources of Hong Kong's emerging human rights picture are as varied as the contextual elements. The idea of 'one country, two systems' embodied in the Joint Declaration envisions an untested model of a liberal capitalist autonomous region within a Marxist-Leninist country. One can expect that the use of diverse sources in devolving the human rights component of this model will produce a hybrid.

The adoption of the International Covenant on Civil and Political Rights as the guiding instrument for both the Basic Law and the Bill of Rights Ordinance, as well as promised adherence to other international human rights covenants, has added further to the diversity of sources. Understanding the fundamental nature of these diverse sources and the tensions involved may facilitate the use of Hong Kong's growing number of human rights instruments in a way consistent with the parties' objectives for Hong Kong.

• *Implementation*: Achieving the parties' objectives for Hong Kong clearly demands a system of judicial review of legislation to implement the requirements of the International Covenant on Civil and Political Rights, both under the Basic Law and the Bill of Rights. This is currently being done under the Hong Kong Bill of Rights Ordinance and the human rights guarantees of the Letters Patent. Given Hong Kong's common law tradition and the use of the International Covenant, with its similarity to the European Convention on Human Rights, reference to diverse sources of precedent has allowed for orderly development of Hong Kong's human rights jurisprudence. Hong Kong would be well advised to maintain the Bill of Rights Ordinance and the elements of this Hong Kong tradition after 1997. At the same time, the creation of a human rights commission and tribunal can allow for specialization and less costly methods to extend human rights protection to the public.

• *Product*: All of these diverse sources for Hong Kong's human rights agenda may give rise to a vigorous and healthy constitutional discourse in the human rights area and may even produce a unique model for securing human rights. At the same time, with vast international experience and universal standards being brought to bear, this process can be stable and orderly. What is most striking about this modern human rights project is its intricate international character and the seemingly magnetic pull of universal standards.

Notes

1. Joint Declaration of the Government of the United Kingdom of Great Britain and Northern Ireland and the Government of the People's Republic of China on the Question of Hong Kong (hereinafter 'Joint Declaration') 1984.

2. International Covenant on Civil and Political Rights, 6 *I.L.M.* 368 (1967); International Covenant on Economic, Social and Cultural Rights, 6 *I.L.M.* 360 (1967) (Britain acceded for itself and all dependencies including Hong Kong on 20 May 1976).
3. Joint Declaration, Article 3, Section 5 and Annex I, Article XIII.
4. *Hong Kong and Human Rights: Flaws in the System*, AI Index: ASA 19/01/94, Distr: SC/CO/PO (London: Amnesty International, 1994).
5. Joint Declaration, Article 3, Section 5.
6. *Ibid*, Annex I, Article II.
7. The Basic Law of the Hong Kong Special Administrative Region of the People's Republic of China (hereinafter 'Basic Law') April, 1990.
8. *Ibid,* Annexes I and II.
9. *Ibid*, Articles 23, 44, 55, 61, 67, 71, 90, and 101.
10. Article 39 of the Basic Law provides:

    The provisions of the International Covenant on Civil and Political Rights, the International Covenant on Economic, Social and Cultural Rights, and international labour conventions as applied to Hong Kong shall remain in force and shall be implemented through the laws of the Hong Kong Special Administrative Region.

    The rights and freedoms enjoyed by Hong Kong residents shall not be restricted unless as prescribed by law. Such restrictions shall not contravene the provisions of the preceding paragraph of this Article.
11. China's Basic Law drafting process involved a Drafting Committee of 58 members and a Basic Law Consultative Committee of 178 members. Thirty-three drafters were from the Mainland while twenty-five were from Hong Kong. All 178 members of the Consultative Committee were from Hong Kong. Initially seven Hong Kong members served on both committees. These various figures changed over time with dismissals, resignations, and deaths.
12. Constitution of the People's Republic of China, Articles 62 and 67.
13. Article 158 of the Basic Law provides:

    The power of interpretation of this Law shall be vested in the Standing Committee of the National People's Congress.

    The Standing Committee of the National People's Congress shall authorize the courts of the Hong Kong Special Administrative Region to interpret on their own, in adjudicating cases, the provisions of this Law which are within the limits of the autonomy of the Region.

    The courts of the Hong Kong Special Administrative Region

may also interpret other provisions of this Law in adjudicating cases. However, if the courts of the Region, in adjudicating cases, need to interpret the provisions of this Law concerning affairs which are the responsibility of the Central People's Government, or concerning the relationship between the Central Authorities and the Region, and if such interpretation will affect the judgments on the cases, the courts of the Region shall, before making their final judgments which are not appealable, seek an interpretation of the relevant provisions from the Standing Committee of the National People's Congress through the Court of Final Appeal of the Region. When the Standing Committee makes an interpretation of the provisions concerned, the courts of the Region, in applying those provisions, shall follow the interpretation of the Standing Committee. However, judgments previously rendered shall not be affected.

The Standing Committee of the National People's Congress shall consult its Committee for the Basic Law of the Hong Kong Special Administrative Region before giving an interpretation of this Law.

14. Article 17 of the Basic Law provides:

The Hong Kong Special Administrative Region shall be vested with legislative power.

Laws enacted by the legislature of the Hong Kong Special Administrative Region must be reported to the Standing Committee of the National People's Congress for the record. The reporting for the record shall not affect the entry into force of such laws.

If the Standing Committee of the National People's Congress, after consulting the Committee for the Basic Law of the Hong Kong Special Administrative Region under it, considers that any law enacted by the legislature of the Region is not in conformity with the provisions of this Law regarding affairs within the responsibility of the Central Authorities or regarding the relationship between the Central Authorities and the Region, the Standing Committee may return the law in question but shall not amend it. Any law returned by the Standing Committee of the National People's Congress shall immediately be invalidated. This invalidation shall not have retroactive effect, unless otherwise provided for in the laws of the Region.

15. In addition to maintenance of the common law system, the Joint Declaration requires that the laws of the Region not contravene the Basic Law, that every person have the right to challenge the actions of the executive in the courts, that the region have a high degree of autonomy, and that local courts exercise power independently, free from interference, and with finality.

The Joint Declaration further provides that laws 'which are in accordance with the Basic Law and legal procedures shall be regarded as valid'.

16. See generally, R. Edwards, L. Henkin, A. Nathan, *Human Rights in Contemporary China*, New York: Columbia University Press, 1986.
17. *Human Rights in China*, Beijing: Information Office of the State Council, 1991.
18. Hong Kong Bill of Rights Ordinance, Ordinance No. 59 (1991).
19. Basic Law, Article 39; Joint Declaration, Annex I, Article XIII.
20. Hong Kong Letters Patent 1991 (No. 2), L.N. 226 of 1991.
21. Hong Kong Bill of Rights Ordinance, Part II, Article 16 (ICCPR Art. 19).
22. A. Byrnes, J. Chan, *Hong Kong Bill of Rights Bulletin*, Vols. 1–4 (1991–95) (reports cases under the Bill of Rights).
23. *R.* v. *Sin Yau-ming* [1992] 1 HKCLR 127, 141–142 (CA).
24. *Attorney General* v. *Lee Kwong-kut; Attorney General* v. *Lo Chak-man* (1993) 3 HKPLR 72, [1993] 3 WLR 242, [1993] 2 All ER 510 (PC)(presumption of innocence, upholding the long-standing common law approach after passage of the Bill of Rights); *Tam Hing-yee* v. *Wu tai-wai* [1992] 1 HKLR 185 (CA); *R.* v. *Kwok Wai-chun* (1992) Mag, FL No. 4305 of 1992 (no exclusionary rule).
25. See, *R.* v. *Lam Tak-ming and Lam Ho-ming* (1992) DCt, DC No. 271 of 1991, in *Bill of Rights Bulletin*, 1, 3, (1992) p. 29.

Why Hong Kong Should Have Equal Opportunities Legislation and a Human Rights Commission

Anna Wu

Human rights should be regarded as universal and fundamental. They should be enjoyed by all individuals. They serve
to protect the strong as well as the most vulnerable members
of society. The degree to which a government is willing to
adhere to these standards reflects the extent of its respect for
its citizens.

In this essay I will highlight some of the current efforts to
secure a full commitment to human rights sufficient for
confidence in Hong Kong's future. In doing so I will discuss
the recent history of neglect of human rights and point out
the inadequacies of the existing system. I will then focus
more directly on the question of equal opportunities and the
need for legislation in this regard. Finally, I will outline the
salient features of legislative proposals which I, as a Member
of the Hong Kong Legislative Council, submitted in early
1994, and the government subsequently rejected, for a Human
Rights and Equal Opportunities Commission.

An overview of these proposals will help to establish a base-
line from which to judge the merits of a human rights commission and point towards the most appropriate avenue for
implementing important human rights commitments by the
Hong Kong government. At the same time this effort may
stand as an example of domestic activity within an Asian
community to better secure human rights protection

A History of Human Rights Neglect

The British Government extended to Hong Kong in 1976
both the International Covenant on Economic, Social and
Cultural Rights and the International Covenant on Civil and
Political Rights.[1] However, it was not until the 1984 signing
of the Joint Declaration of the Government of the United

Kingdom of Great Britain and Northern Ireland and the Government of the People's Republic of China on the Question of Hong Kong (hereinafter 'the Joint Declaration') that the Hong Kong public first became widely aware of the existence of these covenants. These covenants were important enough to warrant special mention in the Joint Declaration and were regarded as sufficiently fundamental to require preservation beyond 1997. Nevertheless, despite the importance of these covenants the British and Hong Kong governments did nothing to promote Hong Kong people's awareness of the rights described in them.

If the future of Hong Kong had not become an issue, these commitments would probably have remained hidden from the Hong Kong public for many years. Insofar as the British Hong Kong Government was concerned, it was assumed that for so long as there was a benevolent colonial administration looking after the welfare of Hong Kong, the public did not need to exercise these rights or, indeed, to know of their existence. The government knew what was best for the public.

More than ten years after these covenants were first disclosed in the Joint Declaration, the British and Hong Kong governments have done little to implement them. In 1988, at a hearing of the United Nations Human Rights Committee, Britain was asked what had been done to promote awareness of the rights under the International Covenant on Civil and Political Rights in Hong Kong — its response: nothing. This attitude on the part of the British and Hong Kong governments showed a blatant disregard for the rights of the people of Hong Kong to know about or participate in any sphere of civil and political rights. Of course, educating the public is tantamount to equipping the public with knowledge to challenge the actions and omissions of government. Clearly the Hong Kong Government did not consider this in its interest. At the very least, an informed public represented an inconvenience the government wished to avoid. It is always easier for a government to keep citizens in the dark.

The 1988 report (presented to the United Nations Human Rights Committee by the British Government) was more notable for what was left out than for what it actually said. It made no mention of newly enacted legislation in Hong Kong promoting political censorship of films, of recently introduced criminal sanctions for the publication of news regarded as false, or of the prohibition against the use of loudhailers (which are required for communication at large public gatherings) without a licence. This report represented the government's selection of only those facts that the government regarded as presenting it in a favourable light.

The apparent tranquility of Hong Kong was disturbed by the June 4th tragedy in Beijing in 1989. In the aftermath of such a cruel abuse of human rights Britain's disowning of six million Hong Kong people — the majority of them British subjects — came under attack. To salvage the situation and to shore up confidence in Hong Kong, the British Government decided to entrench the International Covenant on Civil and Political Rights through domestic legislation in the form of a bill of rights ordinance. Suddenly, people began to realize that human rights should no longer be taken for granted. Ironically, the event that triggered this change of heart occurred in China, not in Hong Kong or Britain.[2]

At the time of the passage of the Hong Kong Bill of Rights Ordinance in 1991, the Chief Secretary of the Hong Kong Government said:

> Sir, we are not embarked on some unique adventure. There are many jurisdictions, particularly in the common law world, with their own charter of rights. It is a feature of almost all Commonwealth jurisdictions. The value of such a law is, I believe, clear: it serves as a yardstick, a focal point, and it is a vital educative tool, bringing home to the consciousness of private individuals and public officials alike the importance of essential rights and freedoms, which in a free society we are always in danger of taking for granted.[2]

If human rights should not be taken for granted and if to legislate to protect human rights is not embarking on a unique adventure, why then did it take the Hong Kong Government so long to do anything? Clearly, it would not do anything to tie its own hands unless it was forced into it.

When I asked the government in the Legislative Council in 1993 whether it would consult the public and hold public hearings before filing future reports of human rights developments in Hong Kong with the United Nations Human Rights Committee, the government declined to answer. When I asked in 1994 if the government would be willing to provide legislators with an advance copy of the human rights report before it was submitted to the United Nations Human

Rights Committee, the response was an unambiguous 'no'. Asked in 1993 whether the government would allow legislators to attend hearings before the United Nations Human Rights Committee as members of the Britain/Hong Kong Government team, the answer again was 'no'.

It is clear that the government does not welcome any view on human rights in Hong Kong other than its own. It is also clear that it does not wish to be challenged in any way. There is no incentive for it to report its own misconduct or to be bound legally by domestic law to implement its international obligations and to subject itself to scrutiny.

The fact of the matter is that there is no one to perform an audit of the performance of the Hong Kong Government and to provide a view as to whether the government has presented a fair and accurate picture of the human rights situation in Hong Kong. The fact of the matter is also that the government would not wish to be obligated to act. This problem is made particularly severe when there is no elected government.

Under the International Covenant for Civil and Political Rights, a member territory has a responsibility not only to respect the rights of the Covenant but also to extend these rights to its citizens. Article 2 of the Covenant requires all parties bound by the Covenant to provide for a process to determine the occurrence of human rights violations, to develop remedies for breaches of human rights, to implement these remedies, and to enforce them. In so doing, the Covenant recognizes that the rights are fundamental to a society and represent the values to which a society aspires. They are regarded as proactive and positive rights. They require a government to commit itself to take active steps to advance the cause of human rights and to give these rights substantive content.

By ratifying the Covenant and extending it to Hong Kong, the British Government, and through it the Hong Kong Government, committed itself to taking initiatives to secure the enjoyment of these rights by the people of Hong Kong. Hong Kong waited for any positive action until 1991 when the Hong Kong Bill of Rights was finally enacted. The language of the Bill of Rights reflects almost word for word the provisions of the International Covenant on Civil and Political Rights.

While the overdue Hong Kong Bill of Rights is laudable, since it finally ensures that the rights under the Covenant are justiciable in the courts of Hong Kong, it is lacking in crucial areas. For instance, it provides no detailed legislation to prohibit discrimination, to protect privacy, and to provide access to information. Without detailed legislation these concepts, though entrenched in the Bill, are not justiciable or enforceable.

The government's delinquency would seem to be particularly egregious in the area of equal opportunities legislation. The Hong Kong Bill of Rights contains broad guarantees against discrimination, but only in a limited context. Article 1 prohibits discrimination with regard to the enjoyment of the rights protected by the Bill of Rights itself. Article 22 provides a more general guarantee of equal protection of the law. However, the effect of these provisions is limited by Section 7 of the Bill of Rights, which states that the Bill of Rights binds only the government and public authorities 'and persons acting on their behalf'.

Thus, the Hong Kong Bill of Rights cannot be used to remedy discrimination by private parties, such as private employers. Furthermore, Section 7 has been interpreted by the Court of Appeal to prevent application of the Bill of Rights to any dispute between private parties, even where one of the parties is relying upon legislation which the other party alleges violates the Bill of Rights (*Tam Hingyee* v. *Wu Taiwai* [1992] 1 HKLR 185). Thus, specific equal opportunities legislation is necessary not only to prevent discriminatory acts by private parties but also to reform discriminatory legislation affecting private relationships and transactions.

The original draft of the proposed Bill of Rights was not so limited. The draft circulated for public comment was expressed to bind public and private persons. However, final legislative changes made shortly before the Bill was enacted amended Section 7, restricting the Bill's application to government and public authorities. The chief government argument made in favour of so limiting the scope of the Bill of Rights was that issues like discrimination in the private sector would be better dealt with by specific legislation than by the general provision of the Hong Kong Bill of Rights. It was at least implied that once the Bill of Rights was enacted, the Hong Kong Government would give serious consideration to legislation prohibiting discrimination in the public and private sectors.

Three years down the road the Government has done virtually nothing to provide substantive content to the broad principles under the Bill of Rights or to supplement its inadequacies. No comprehensive and detailed equal opportunities legislation has been proposed; nor have proposals been forthcoming for the protection of privacy or to provide legally assured access to government information.

In June 1994, three months after I publicized my proposals for Equal Opportunities legislation and a Human Rights and Equal Opportunities Commission for Hong Kong, the government most grudgingly announced its legislative proposal to deal with sex discrimination. The proposal covers the narrowest possible conception of sex discrimination, without reference to discrimination on the grounds of pregnancy, marital status, or discrimination against single parents and omits any protection against discrimination on other grounds, such as age, race, or sexuality. The proposal also would establish a commission which is essentially a conciliation service for sex discrimination cases and is confined by a narrow, legalistic notion of women's rights.

The government introduced the Sex Discrimination Bill in October 1994. Reacting to pressure, the Bill is slightly wider than originally contemplated by the government. However, the government's intended postponement of the law's implementation until after codes of practice have been promulgated, and the many significant exemptions, cast doubt on the government's sincerity.

In the same month, the government also announced a proposal for administrative measures that would provide for access to government information, but rejected legislators' calls for legislation. While conceding that the public should have access to government information, it denies the public the legal right under statute to secure it and to penalize the government for omissions and failures.

When the Bill of Rights was enacted, legislators and the government recognized that there were prior laws in Hong Kong which were inconsistent with Hong Kong's obligations under the International Covenant for Civil and Political Rights. A Legislative Council Committee had identified over 50 laws thought to be in possible conflict with the Bill of

Rights. The Hong Kong Bill of Rights provided a freeze period of one year (subsequently extended to two) for certain laws such as those relating to the powers of the Independent Commission Against Corruption and the police. Clearly, it was expected that these would be reviewed and brought in line with the Bill of Rights. While those specifically excluded from the immediate application of the Bill of Rights were more easily ascertainable, there were, in addition, other laws which would be immediately affected by the Bill of Rights. With regard to these laws which require review, amendment, or repeal, we are nowhere close to finishing the exercise of identification and amendment or repeal.

There have been ongoing arguments between liberal groups and the government as to whether there are violations of Hong Kong's international human rights obligations. One such area is the political censorship of films, where a censor could require excision of any part of a film if it was likely to cause damage to Hong Kong's good relations with neighbouring territories. The matter was never tested in court and certainly, if that had happened, an interpretation in accordance with the international norms would have been made. The relevant provision required that the standards applied must take into account the obligations under Article 19 of the International Covenant on Civil and Political Rights. The power to censor films for political reasons has now been removed by the Film Censorship (Amendment) Ordinance, which was initiated by legislator Martin Lee, and enacted as law in December 1994.

Other areas also badly need reform and clarification. These have included a New Territories ordinance which deprived indigenous women of land inheritance rights, the interception of incoming or outgoing telecommunication messages, and restrictions relating to media freedom, assembly and the use of loudhailers, and the conduct and treatment of prisoners and detainees. The infamous New Territories ordinance was finally amended in June 1994 with the removal of the prohibition against indigenous women inheriting rural land. The government has also introduced some legislative modifications to the laws relating to public processions, public meetings, and the use of loudhailers. These measures have been adopted as a result of pressure from the public and the Legislative Council.

The government remains passive in areas of law reform required as a consequence of the Bill of Rights. In June 1994, a government case concerning the presumption of possession of drugs was thrown out of court for violating the Bill of Rights. This case further tarnished the image and credibility of our police. The police have imposed upon themselves a moratorium on a number of laws which they fear to be unenforceable. The government should actively be reviewing these laws and looking for more palatable substitutes.

Where existing laws are in conflict with the Bill of Rights, these laws, until amended, remain on the statute books causing a lot of uncertainty. They also represent areas of potential abuse of power by the government because the public is left to the mercy of the government which exercises its discretion in deciding what the interpretation should be. Where the government is unwilling to state its position on a law, its solution has been to leave it to the courts. The question is: how many cases calling these laws into question will ever get to court, and how long will the process take?

The Amnesty International report entitled 'Hong Kong and Human Rights: Flaws in the System', released on 21 April 1994, summarized the shortcomings of the current judicial system as follows:

• People who have wished to bring civil cases against the Hong Kong public authorities for Bill of Rights violations have been deterred by the cost. Such cases can be extremely expensive and people have often been refused legal aid.
• The formality, complexity, and slowness of the Hong Kong court system deter people from bringing civil cases against the government on Bill of Rights issues. Delays have become a serious problem. The wait is still longer when the government appeals decisions against it.
• Civil cases raising Bill of Rights issues have rarely been brought against the Hong Kong Government. The few on record have tended to be brought by commercial interests who can afford the costs, with Bill of Rights issues somewhat marginal to the cases.[3]

The same report went on to state that between June 1991 (when the Hong Kong Bill of Rights came into effect) and 30 November 1993, over 92 per cent of applications for legal aid in Bill of Rights civil cases (excluding immigration cases) were rejected under the 'merit test' of the Legal Aid Department.

Currently, there is no channel to test the validity of laws, even if a significant point of human rights is involved, before damage is done, and legal aid may not always be available to the victim due to the stringent merit test in place. The law, even where it provides redress, is beyond the reach of the average person, especially when one considers the potential risk of the local 'loser-pays-all' system which tends to discourage claims.

It is not a respectable system if there is no certainty to the law and if protection of human rights is not secured or enforceable. The government's inertia in the area of human rights protection is startling. If we are to uphold human rights in any way meaningful, that task must be entrusted to a separate body that can promote and provide protection where the government is either unwilling or unable to do so. After all, it must be borne in mind that one of the major areas of friction is the protection of the individual against the political excesses of the state. Even if the government is not itself a party to a dispute over rights, it is an unreliable guardian given self-confessed 'competing priorities'.

The Need for Equal Opportunities Legislation

Against this background in 1994 I proposed equal opportunities legislation and a Human Rights and Equal Opportunities Commission for Hong Kong. There are compelling reasons for introducing these measures. Comprehensive equal opportunities legislation is desirable as a means of maintaining social justice and human rights and adhering to Hong Kong's international obligations. Such legislation can also provide tangible benefits for the people of Hong Kong.

Eleanor Roosevelt, who chaired the committee that drafted the Universal Declaration of Human Rights, said that human rights begin at home:

> In small places, close to home — so close and so small that they cannot be seen on any map of the world. Yet they are the world of the individual person. The neighbourhood he lives in; the school or college he attends; the factory, farm or office where he works. Such are the places where

every man, woman and child seeks equal justice, equal
opportunity, equal dignity without discrimination. Unless
these rights have meaning there, they have little meaning
anywhere. Without concerted citizen action to uphold them
close to home, we shall look in vain for progress in the
larger world.[4]

It is difficult to imagine what better ways exist to ensure
each man, woman, and child in Hong Kong has an equal
measure of protection before the law and an equal measure
of opportunity than the enactment of equal opportunities
legislation and the setting up of a human rights and equal
opportunities commission.

There is significant evidence that discrimination causes real
hardship in Hong Kong and that it is not disappearing on
its own. For example, there can be no question that women
in the New Territories suffer financially and politically from
sexual discrimination. Often this is the result of the enforcement of customary practices that have been abolished in
other Chinese societies — and which probably would have
been reformed here as well had they not been 'frozen in
time' by colonial ordinances. Women in the New Territories
are ineligible to apply for the indigenous residents' 'small
house' entitlement (a government housing programme which
is excluded from the application of the proposed Sex Discrimination Bill) and up until 1994 were still prohibited from
inheriting most land in the New Territories. Moreover, in
one-third of the villages in the New Territories, women are
not even permitted to stand for election as Village Representatives. Their right to vote in these elections is also curtailed:
some villages permit only males to vote, while others permit only the head of household to vote, effectively excluding most women.

The workplace provides many examples of unfair discriminatory practices. The classified sections of any Hong Kong
newspaper run advertisements seeking applicants of a particular sex and age. They regularly seek 'male-only' applicants
for managerial and professional positions and 'female-only'
applicants for low-paid clerical positions. Moreover, government statistics demonstrate that even when men and women
are employed in precisely the same positions, women are,
on average, paid significantly less than their male counterparts for exactly the same work. As of this writing there are

still no laws against employment policies which discriminate on the basis of sex, although, following the introduction of my Equal Opportunities Bill, the Sex Discrimination Bill has been introduced by government — both are under review by a Bills committee of the Legislative Council. Employers are also still free to discriminate on the basis of race, religion, or age. In addition to causing hardship to the victims, such discrimination also hurts the Hong Kong economy, for it discourages those who are denied equal opportunities from working harder and realizing their full potential. It may also mean that employers fail to employ the person most qualified for a particular job.

Handicapped people also need better equal opportunities protection. Recent attempts by the government to open facilities for handicapped children in the community have been met by threats of violence by some communities. The mentally disabled are members of our community and are entitled to basic human dignity, access to services, and the opportunity to lead a fulfilling life — just like other members of society. But the historical absence of laws against discrimination has left them vulnerable to prejudice, cruelty, and a simple lack of respect. The physically disabled, the elderly, and those infected with the HIV/AIDS virus are similarly vulnerable. This is particularly true of individuals who, as the result of increased emigration from Hong Kong, find themselves without the protection of an extended family.

There have also been many reports of racial discrimination in Hong Kong. In some cases this takes the form of unjustifiably less favourable terms for 'local' employees. (The term 'local' is often interpreted to include people who are not from Hong Kong but are Chinese.) In other cases, the discrimination is against non-Chinese groups (such as Indians and Filipinos) who have for many years played a very important and positive role in the Hong Kong economy.

Indeed, even the Hong Kong Government, which should be sensitive to the importance of treating all citizens equally, sometimes fails to uphold this principle. For example, the Labour Department recently posted advertisements for clerical positions in government departments which specified age limitations (such as: '20–35', '20–30', and even '17–24'). Such discrimination is particularly harmful to women, as they are more likely than men to leave the labour market temporarily to bear children. When they return, they face these advertisements (which are also very prevalent in the private sector). Yet, clearly, there is no reason why women in their 30s, 40s, and 50s should be prohibited from applying for these positions.

Under a number of international treaties applicable to Hong Kong, the United Kingdom has assumed obligations to take effective steps to eradicate discrimination of various sorts and to provide effective remedies under Hong Kong law. In some cases, the desirability of legislation or even its necessity is made clear in the treaty, or in the practice of the supervisory bodies established by the treaty. A good faith interpretation of those treaties compels the conclusion that there must be legislation making discrimination unlawful and providing for effective and adequate remedies.

The main treaties of relevance are the International Convention on the Elimination of All Forms of Racial Discrimination (applicable to Hong Kong since 1969)[5], the International Covenant on Civil and Political Rights (applicable since 1976), and the International Covenant on Economic, Social and Cultural Rights (also applicable since 1976). Detailed legislation covering both public and private racial discrimination is required by the Racial Discrimination Convention, while more general legislation covering both public and private discrimination on the grounds of race, sex, and impairment, among other things, is required by the two International Covenants. The failure to enact such legislation — despite continuing discrimination in these areas — (eighteen years since the Covenants entered into force in Hong Kong) constitutes a failure to carry out the obligations accepted under those treaties by the British and Hong Kong governments.

A Human Rights and Equal Opportunities Commission

The ideal mechanism for dealing with allegations of discrimination (other than cases in which the validity of legislation may be at issue) would be a procedure that seeks to bring about an amicable agreement between the parties that respects the human rights involved. In drafting a private member's bill (a bill proposed by a legislator, as opposed to a bill proposed by the government) in Hong Kong in 1994, my colleagues and I tried to identify certain preferred characterics for such legislation in a society with Hong Kong's common law legal system and social conditions. Our proposal may provide a standard by which to judge legislative initiatives in this area. The reasoning behind the proposal we presented to the government for consideration is discussed below.

Under the draft Human Rights and Equal Opportunities Commission Bill that we proposed for Hong Kong, complaints of discrimination would be required to be lodged with an independent Human Rights and Equal Opportunities Commission (similar to commissions established in common law countries such as Australia and Canada).

The advantages of this procedure, as opposed to going through the ordinary courts, are many. The more informal procedure and congenial environment are more conducive to resolving discrimination claims. Litigation in the courts (even if one is successful) is expensive and time-consuming, and takes place in a formal adversarial environment. The proposed commission would also be responsible for investigating complaints relating to human rights violations and attempting conciliation between the parties. Finally, the commission would be complemented by a tribunal to which the complaints which resist conciliation could be referred for adjudication, with an appeal on questions of law to the higher courts. This latter feature would ensure that the role of developing legal precedent, in the common law tradition, is maintained and encouraged.

The functions of this proposed Human Rights and Equal Opportunities Commission would go well beyond processing complaints. The effective implementation of human rights guarantees in Hong Kong requires an independent commission to undertake a broad range of functions including education, research, and community liaison, as well as review of government programmes and of existing and proposed legislation, and advising the government. The proposed commission would also have the power to initiate proceedings in certain circumstances and to intervene in proceedings in which important human rights issues are being considered.

Some have expressed concerns that an easily accessible commission would increase the incidence of complaints and intensify disputes. This is reading the problems backwards. In the absence of appropriate legislation, many cases of discrimination go unremedied, and Hong Kong pays a social cost for not recognizing the problem. An effective enforcement mechanism helps parties to a dispute to attempt meaningful conciliation and voluntary changes. It provides the incentive to change, to adjust, and to self-correct.

There have also been concerns that a human rights and equal opportunities commission would duplicate the functions of several channels of redress and thus create institutional redundancy. Various complaint channels, such as the Commission Against Maladministration and the complaints division of the Legislative Council may occasionally touch on human rights concerns. Similarly, the government has added human rights to the agenda of the Committee on the Promotion of Civic Education, and placed human rights under the portfolio of the Secretary of Home Affairs.

None of these bodies, however, focuses on all related aspects of human rights. The current approach, instead, splits up the human rights problem and distributes it across a variety of organizations, none of which is dedicated to human rights issues as its principal concern. Thus, complaints handling is severed from education about human rights. Continuing this fragmented approach would also slow down the development of standards, policy, and solutions. Protection of human rights should not be a peripheral or a fragmented exercise.

The Independent Commission Against Corruption, for instance, represents a focused commitment and a targeted approach to dealing comprehensively with the problem of corruption. In terms of institutional overlap, there is nothing that this commission can do which cannot be undertaken by another institution of the government. To develop human rights systematically and comprehensively requires a similar commitment. Unfortunately, there is little resemblance between the government's growing concerns about corruption and its concerns about human rights laws. Human rights represent an even more fundamental social commitment and, if they are to be taken seriously, require a comparable autonomous implementing body.

One of the most important aspects of the development of human rights in any territory is the development of standards, both of implementation and interpretation. These standards should be set by a body outside the government. It is obvious that they should not be left to the government alone. The standard-setting function can help Hong Kong to build up jurisprudence consistent with international norms. It also can help Hong Kong to legislate more precisely to meet such standards.

Given the track record of the Hong Kong Government in the area of human rights development, it should not be at all difficult to conclude that what Hong Kong needs is an authoritative and independent human rights commission that will develop human rights awareness and protection in an objective fashion. It should have the authority to do the following:

* monitor government policies and programmes,
* provide advice on legislation and other human rights matters,
* promote awareness of human rights and educate the public,
* provide reports on human rights development in Hong Kong to international supervisory bodies,
* investigate complaints,
* provide dispute settlement on matters relating to human rights,
* provide legal expertise and financial assistance to complainants initiating proceedings relating to human rights violations,
* help develop jurisprudence and standards of interpretation relating to human rights in Hong Kong in a manner consistent with international norms, and
* initiate proceedings to clarify the status of laws which may be inconsistent with Hong Kong's international obligations and domestic laws relating to human rights such as the Hong Kong Bill of Rights.

Conclusion

In the proposal for the establishment of a human rights and equal opportunities commission, we included the following functions, which might have served as standards by which to judge any human rights or equal opportunities commission established:

1. Educational and promotional functions. This is a central and indispensable role of any human rights commission. The commission should have the task of disseminating information about human rights and of promoting respect for the observance of these human rights in Hong Kong. The commission should also work to develop guidelines or codes of conduct for particular sectors of the community. The commission can thereby play an important preventive or proactive role in working with institutions to bring about systematic changes.

2. Research and advisory functions. In addition to the research necessary to develop educational programmes, a human rights commission should have a number of research and advisory duties relating to law and policy making. The commission may prepare reports on laws that the government should make or actions which the government should take. The commission should examine existing laws or propose laws when a request to do so is made by the Attorney General, by the President of the Legislative Council, or by any 500 persons living in Hong Kong and should also examine international treaties or other instruments that have not been extended to Hong Kong. The commission may provide information to the international supervisory bodies associated with international instruments affecting Hong Kong. The commission may also intervene in any proceedings relating to human rights. This can enable the commission to assist the court in interpreting and developing human rights in Hong Kong, in light of the growing body of relevant comparative and international jurisprudence.

3. Resolution of complaints functions. A human rights commission may inquire into acts or practices which appear to be inconsistent with human rights standards, and may endeavour by conciliation to achieve a settlement of such matters. The commission may carry out an investigation to ascertain the facts and may demand the production of information. If conciliation is unsuccessful, and if the commission considers it appropriate at any stage to do so, the commissioner may refer the complaint to the tribunal for adjudication. The commission may be empowered to provide financial assistance to a complainant both before the tribunal and on appeal to the court.

4. Adjudication functions. The powers and the procedures of the tribunal are those of a District Court. The tribunal may formulate its own procedural rules and may in certain cases dispense with technicalities and legal form. It may, for instance, conduct hearings in an informal manner and take account of statistical evidence. The tribunal may make orders for reinstatement in the case of actions under the proposed equal opportunities legislation, award compensation or punitive damages, issue restraining orders, and exercise judicial review to declare laws or official actions inconsistent with certain human rights requirements, such as those in the Hong Kong Bill of Rights or the proposed equal opportunities legislation. The appeal against a decision of the tribunal may be made on a point of law to the Court of Appeal.

5. Initiation and exemption functions. The commission may initiate proceedings in its own name, in the tribunal or any other court of competent jurisdiction, in certain circumstances:

• if it appears to the commission that an act which is unlawful under the Bill of Rights or the proposed equal opportunities legislation may have been committed by the government, by a public authority, or by a person exercising a power conferred by law or executive prerogative; or

• if it appears to the commission that a legislative provision or rule of the common law is inconsistent with, or has been repealed by, the Bill of Rights, the proposed equal opportunities legislation, or Article VII(3) of the Hong Kong Letters Patent (which constitutionally entrenches the International Covenant on Civil and Political Rights as part of the law of Hong Kong).

This would provide important advantages in clarifying the status of the laws with regard to those which might be inconsistent with human rights standards and require the government to rectify problems before further human rights violations result.

The commission would also be empowered to grant to applicants an exemption from specified provisions of the proposed equal opportunities legislation for a specified (but renewable) term. Other interested parties may make submissions to the commission during consideration of applications for such exemptions. If aggrieved by the commission's decision, an applicant or such other parties as have made submissions, may appeal to the tribunal.

The other essayists in this book have discussed the numerous difficulties associated with the achievement of human rights in Asia and particularly in China. The absence of sufficient legal institutions and the rule of law has been a glaring problem. With many legal institutions already in place, Hong Kong's evolving human rights regime offers the opportunity to transcend many of the difficulties evident elsewhere and firmly establish an 'Asian' example of commitment to human rights. The current Hong Kong government, in particular, can avail itself of this opportunity before Hong Kong confronts the widely acknowledged uncertainty of 1997. The Bill of Rights was a good first step; a human rights and equal opportunities commission, as proposed in this essay, is a needed second step to establish fully a commitment to human rights and the rule of law in Hong Kong. We can only hope that our community has the will to seize this opportunity before it slips away.

Notes

1. International Covenant on Civil and Political Rights, 6 *I.L.M.* 368 (1967); International Covenant on Economic, Social and Cultural Rights, 6 *I.L.M.* 360 (1967). Britain acceded on behalf of Hong Kong on 20 May 1976.
2. Chief Secretary's Speech on the presentation of the Bill of Rights Ordinance, Hong Kong Legislative Council, 5 June 1991.
3. Summary of the report entitled 'Hong Kong and Human Rights: Flaws in the System', London: Amnesty International, 21 April 1994.
4. 'Teaching Human Rights', New York: United Nations, 1963, p. 1.
5. Convention on the Elimination of All Forms of Racial Discrimination, 5 *I.L.M.* 352 (1964).

Appendix

The Bangkok Declaration

The Ministers and representatives of Asian States, meeting at Bangkok from 29 March to 2 April 1993, pursuant to General Assembly resolution 46/116 of 17 December 1991 in the context of preparations for the World Conference on Human Rights,

Adopt this Declaration, to be known as 'The Bangkok Declaration', which contains the aspirations and commitments of the Asian region:

Bangkok Declaration

Emphasizing the significance of the World Conference on Human Rights, which provides an invaluable opportunity to review all aspects of human rights and ensure a just and balanced approach thereto,

Recognizing the contribution that can be made to the World Conference by Asian countries with their diverse and rich cultures and traditions,

Welcoming the increased attention being paid to human rights in the international community,

Reaffirming their commitment to principles contained in the Charter of the United Nations and the Universal Declaration on Human Rights,

Recalling that in the Charter of the United Nations the question of universal observance and promotion of human rights and fundamental freedoms has been rightly placed within the context of international cooperation,

Noting the progress made in the codification of human rights instruments, and in the establishment of international human rights mechanisms, while *expressing concern* that these mechanisms relate mainly to one category of rights,

Emphasizing that ratification of international human rights instruments, particularly the International Covenant on Civil and Political Rights and the International Covenant on Economic, Social, and Cultural Rights, by all States should be further encouraged,

Reaffirming the principles of respect for national sovereignty, territorial integrity and non-interference in the international affairs of States,

Stressing the universality, objectivity and non-selectivity of all human rights and the need to avoid the application of double standards in the implementation of human rights and its politicization,

Recognizing that the promotion of human rights should be encouraged by cooperation and consensus, and not through confrontation and the imposition of incompatible values,

Reiterating the interdependence and indivisibility of economic, social, cultural, civil and political rights, and the inherent interrelationship between development, democracy, universal enjoyment of all human rights, and social justice which must be addressed in an integrated and balanced manner,

Recalling that the Declaration on the Right to Development has recognized the right to development as a universal and inalienable right and an integral part of fundamental human rights,

Emphasizing that endeavours to move towards the creation of uniform international human rights norms must go hand in hand with endeavours to work towards a just and fair world economic order,

Convinced that economic and social progress facilitates the growing trend towards democracy and the promotion and protection of human rights,

Stressing the importance of education and training in human rights at the national, regional and international levels and the need for international cooperation aimed at overcoming the lack of public awareness of human rights:

1. *Reaffirm* their commitment to the principles contained in the Charter of the United Nations and the Universal Declaration on Human Rights as well as the full realization of all human rights throughout the world;

2. *Underline* the essential need to create favourable conditions for effective enjoyment of human rights at both the national and international levels;

3. *Stress* the urgent need to democratize the United Nations system, eliminate selectivity and improve procedures and mechanisms in order to strengthen international cooperation, based on principles of equality and mutual respect, and ensure a positive, balanced and non-confrontational approach in addressing and realizing all aspects of human rights;

4. *Discourage* any attempt to use human rights as a conditionality for extending development assistance;

5. *Emphasize* the principles of respect for national sovereignty and territorial integrity as well as non-interference in the internal affairs of States, and the non-use of human rights as an instrument of political pressure;

6. *Reiterate* that all countries, large and small, have the right to determine their political systems, control and freely utilize their resources, and freely pursue their economic, social and cultural development;

7. *Stress* the universality, objectivity and non-selectivity of all human rights and the need to avoid the application of double standards in the implementation of human rights and its politicization, and that no violation of human rights can be justified;

8. *Recognize* that while human rights are universal in nature, they must be considered in the context of a dynamic and evolving process

of international norm-setting, bearing in mind the significance of national and regional particularities and various historical, cultural and religious backgrounds;

9. *Recognize further* that States have the primary responsibility for the promotion and protection of human rights through appropriate infrastructure and mechanisms, and also recognize that remedies must be sought and provided primarily through such mechanisms and procedures;

10. *Reaffirm* the interdependence and indivisibility of economic, social, cultural, civil and political rights, and the need to give equal emphasis to all categories of human rights;

11. *Emphasize* the importance of guaranteeing the human rights and fundamental freedoms of vulnerable groups such as ethnic, national, racial, religious and linguistic minorities, migrant workers, disabled persons, indigenous peoples, refugees and displaced persons;

12. *Reiterate* that self-determination is a principle of international law and a universal right recognized by the United Nations for peoples under alien or colonial domination or foreign occupation, by virtue of which they can freely determine their political status and freely pursue their economic, social and cultural development, and that its denial constitutes a grave violation of human rights;

13. *Stress* that the right to self-determination is applicable to peoples under alien or colonial domination or foreign occupation, and should not be used to undermine the territorial integrity, national sovereignty and political independence of States;

14. *Express concern* over all forms of violation of human rights, including manifestations of racial discrimination, racism, apartheid, colonialism, foreign aggression and occupation, and the establishment of illegal settlements in occupied territories, as well as the recent resurgence of neonazism, xenophobia and ethnic cleansing;

15. *Underline* the need for taking effective international measures in order to guarantee and monitor the implementation of human rights standards and effective and legal protection of people under foreign occupation;

16. *Strongly affirm* their support for the legitimate struggle of the Palestinian people to restore their national and inalienable rights to self-determination and independence, and demand an immediate end to the grave violations of human rights in the Palestinian, Syrian Golan and other occupied Arab territories including Jerusalem;

17. *Reaffirm* the right to development, as established in the Declaration on the Right to Development, as a universal and inalienable right and an integral part of fundamental human rights, which must be realized through international cooperation, respect for fundamental human rights, the establishment of a monitoring mechanism and the creation of essential international conditions for the realization of such right;

18. *Recognize* that the main obstacles to the realization of the right to development lie at the international macroeconomic level, as reflected in the widening gap between the North and South, the rich and the poor;

19. *Affirm* that poverty is one of the major obstacles hindering the full enjoyment of human rights;

20. *Affirm also* the need to develop the right of humankind regarding a clean, safe and healthy environment;

21. *Note* that terrorism, in all its forms and manifestations, as distinguished from the legitimate struggle of people under colonial or alien domination or foreign occupation, has emerged as one of the most dangerous threats to the enjoyment of human rights and democracy, threatening the territorial integrity and security of States and destabilizing legitimately constituted governments, and that it must be unequivocally condemned by the international community;

22. *Reaffirm* their strong commitment to the promotion and protection of the right of women through the guarantee of equal participation in the political, social, economic and cultural concerns of society, and the eradication of all forms of discrimination and of gender-based violence against women;

23. *Recognize* the rights of the child to enjoy special protection and to be afforded the opportunities and facilities to develop physically, mentally, morally, spiritually and socially in a healthy and normal manner and in conditions of freedom and dignity;

24. *Welcome* the important role played by national institutions in the genuine and constructive promotion of human rights, and believe that the conceptualization and eventual establishment of such institutions are best left for the States to decide;

25. *Acknowledge* the importance of cooperation and dialogue between governments and non-governmental organizations on the basis of shared values as well as mutual respect and understanding in the promotion of human rights, and encourage the non-governmental organizations in consultative status with the Economic and Social Council to contribute positively to this process in accordance with Council resolution 1296 (XLIV);

26. *Reiterate* the need to explore the possibilities of establishing regional arrangements for the promotion and protection of human rights in Asia;

27. *Reiterate* further the need to explore ways to generate international cooperation and financial support for education and training in the field of human rights at the national level and for the establishment of national infrastructures to promote and protect human rights if requested by States;

28. *Emphasize* the necessity to rationalize the United Nations human rights mechanism in order to enhance its effectiveness and efficiency and the need to ensure avoidance of the duplication of work that

exists between the treaty bodies, the Sub-Commission on Prevention of Discrimination and Protection of Minorities and the Commission on Human Rights, as well as the need to avoid the multiplicity of parallel mechanisms;

29. *Stress* the importance of strengthening the United Nations Centre for Human Rights with the necessary resources to enable it to provide a wide range of advisory services and technical assistance programmes in the promotion of human rights to requesting States in a timely and effective manner, as well as to enable it to finance adequately other activities in the field of human rights authorized by competent bodies;

30. *Call for* increased representation of the developing countries in the Centre for Human Rights.

Index

A common picture of the international human rights debate in the 1990s has the West (notably the US) in a one-sided struggle against the East (especially China), with a great cross-fire of Western accusations and Eastern denials. The ultimate denial is a rejection by some Asian governments of Western standards of protection and the very notion of 'universal human rights'. These are portrayed at worst as alien constructs — the imposition of which amounts to cultural imperialism — and at best as lofty ideas still unattainable.

This picture belies the complexity of the intellectual dialogue within China, and by Chinese overseas, about the legal, philosophical, and political issues surrounding human rights. This book of essays offers a new window onto the emerging Chinese debate.

Are human rights alien to Chinese culture and attitudes? Mainland scholars Du Gangjian and Song Gang look to Confucianism to develop an indigenous Chinese human rights theory. Yu Haocheng assesses current Chinese law and practice, and argues that national sovereignty should not override international human rights concerns. Zhu Feng pins hope for progress to gradual domestic policy changes in China. Hong Kong legislator Christine Loh rejects the cultural relativism echoed in the 1993 Bangkok Declaration, and critically reviews the lurching United Nations human rights process. Each writer invites us to reflect on the practical and theoretical difficulties of the Chinese human rights process and inspires us to explore further.

Michael C. Davis, a senior lecturer in law, is director of the Chinese Law Programme at the Chinese University of Hong Kong, and Schell Senior Fellow at Yale Law School's Schell Center for International Human Rights.

These essays readably, forcefully, intelligently lay out that side of the debate which has so far not received a strong statement in the Asian context. ... This helps break up the fallacy that all Westerners are ranged on one side of this issue and all Asians on the other.

Andrew Nathan
Director, East Asian Institute
Columbia University

ISBN 0-19-586782-3

9 780195 867824